CW00953921

Rose is 29 years old and lives in London. Since graduating in English she's been working as a freelance writer, creating feature articles, short film scripts, short stories and ad concepts. Rose's work has been published by The *Guardian*, The *Independent*, Vice and *Somesuch Stories*. Pure is her first book.

Pure

Rose Bretécher

unbound

unbound

This edition first published in 2015

Unbound
4–7 Manchester Street Marylebone London w1u 2ae
www.unbound.co.uk
All rights reserved

© Rose Bretécher, 2015

Typeset by Ellipsis Digital Limited, Glasgow

Art direction by Mecob

A CIP record for this book
is available from the British Library

ISBN 978–1–78352–112–8 (trade hbk)
ISBN 978–1–78352–166–1 (ebook)
ISBN 978–1–78352–113–5(limited edition)

Printed and bound in England by Clays Ltd, St Ives plc

For Guy

Disclaimer

To respect the privacy of the people mentioned in this book I have changed the names and identifying characteristics of some individuals and locations.

I have had no medical training. The information in this book is based on my personal experiences and understanding, and should not be used as a substitute for qualified medical advice.

Dear Reader,

The book you are holding came about in a rather different way to most others. It was funded directly by readers through a new website: **Unbound**.

Unbound is the creation of three writers. We started the company because we believed there had to be a better deal for both writers and readers. On the Unbound website, authors share the ideas for the books they want to write directly with readers. If enough of you support the book by pledging for it in advance, we produce a beautifully bound special subscribers' edition and distribute a regular edition and e-book wherever books are sold, in shops and online.

This new way of publishing is actually a very old idea (Samuel Johnson funded his dictionary this way). We're just using the internet to build each writer a network of patrons. Here, at the back of this book, you'll find the names of all the people who made it happen.

Publishing in this way means readers are no longer just passive consumers of the books they buy, and authors are free to write the books they really want. They get a much fairer return too – half the profits their books generate, rather than a tiny percentage of the cover price.

If you're not yet a subscriber, we hope that you'll want to join our publishing revolution and have your name listed in one of our books in the future. To get you started, here is a £5 discount on your first pledge. Just visit unbound.com, make your pledge and type **pure** in the promo code box when you check out.

Thank you for your support,

Dan, Justin and John
Founders, Unbound

Pure

'Call the world if you please "The vale of Soul-making". There may be intelligences or sparks of the divinity in millions, but they are not Souls till they acquire identities, till each one is personally itself. Intelligences are atoms of perception – they know and they see and they are pure.'

John Keats, 1819

'We all have the good thoughts and the bad thoughts. Nobody ever expresses the bad thoughts. But the bad thoughts are funny.'

Larry David, 2005

Part One

Pink Velour

I walked down Oxford Street on a hot, hot day in July. Nymph-like girls filed into American Apparel, drawn to the window display of wicker hats and hotpants like wasps to spilt jam. Teenagers, fey with sunshine, smoked outside HMV boasting hard-earned CDs and snogging. I saw a large pair of tits in a lingerie shop window, and winced.

On Wardour Street I met my film producer friend, Erik. I never know whether to kiss twice or not, having grazed many an elderly manboob in the bumbled continental greetings of my half-French childhood, but this was Soho, WeAreSoho, so we kissed on each cheek with obligatory affectation before blinking into the pub. Standing rigid at the bar I watched the white froth in the glasses as the barman gripped the shiny-round tip of the beer tap. Behind us, London's media darlings buzzed with self-conscious chatter.

We cheersed drinks and I did the polite one-sip-and-smile before heading to the bathroom. I didn't need to go, but I had those big, be-lingeried breasts to mull over, and my arousal levels to check. I closed the toilet lid and sat down, and picked at a patch of flaky paint on the door frame. *Did noticing those tits mean I liked them? Like, REALLY liked them? Did the wince-y feeling mean I was INTO them?* I tossed about the yeas and nays for as long as I thought I could get away with, before taking a deep breath and heading back outside. 'No – it meant nothing,' I whispered, as I blinked into the sunlight.

I downed my pint with characteristic speed. I was happy to let my friends assume that my gusto for booze was born of an irrepressible party spirit, when really I was medicating – alcohol made the thoughts less intense. Having long ago noticed this proclivity, my oldest friend Jack had taken to calling me 'Vodderz' in an ironic doff of the hat to the LAD culture which was rearing its pimpled face in every corner of the UK, though how it was ironic neither of us were entirely sure, because when we were pissed together, we were as lairy and objectionable as any Boyz-On-Tour.

Erik and I walked down through Chinatown, where candy-coloured lanterns tinselled the streets and strippers smoked in baking doorways. Kids cast guilty glances into sex shop windows while their parents fumbled nervously with oversized maps on street corners. I looked at the ground when we passed them.

As we wandered down Charing Cross Road, Erik started talking about a new project he had on the horizon – a travel doc about driving across the world. He talked over my 'wow' as we entered Trafalgar Square, where loose-tied workers lazed on the steps and children played in the fountains, fanning the sunset into waterspray rainbows.

Against one fountain's edge, a tourist in a pink velour tracksuit bent to tie her lace, and as I walked behind her, glancing at her giant, cartoon arse, I saw the image of her vagina flash through her trousers, and I flinched, violently, breaking eye contact with Erik and looking at the ground. There it flashed again in a strong, single pulse of photographic clarity, pink and folded and velveteen, and big, as big as the flagstones.

I put on my sunglasses as we walked towards the Strand, scared that someone would see it in my eyes, and clenched my jaw to try to lock it out. But through his words it came, more forcefully this time, flickering more quickly and seeming to distend and darken. In front of us a cloud of pigeons flapped up, clapping into the sky, and in their shivering grey swell I saw it again. The flesh thickened around my throat. *No. No. No,* I said silently, over and over, trying to create a thought-wall to stop the image getting in, but already the screaming had started in the back of my head.

Why did I see that?

Did I like it?

Did I really, REALLY like it?

Now I had to find out. I had to check. I didn't want to but I *had* to, I was utterly compelled. So I looked behind me, back onto Trafalgar Square, and tried to pick out the pink tourist amid the crowds, discreetly, not wanting to arouse suspicion, yet thoroughly unable to resist this huge, compulsive urgency to see that woman again and determine how, *exactly,* I'd felt when that image had burned through her pants, and what, exactly, it'd meant. But she was gone.

It meant nothing, I said again to myself, and so enflamed the image further, making it heave and become stronger still. When I closed my eyes or looked at the fag-flecked tarmac, I saw it again, fifty times, one hundred times, burning bigger by the second, pulsing quicker with each breath I took, becoming a watermark on my vision, violating this beautiful summer's day with its huge, grisly imprint. Now Erik was saying stuff about the Middle East, about India, about amazing adventures, and I tried to focus as he chatted on, but the giant insect in my chest was closing its legs around my lungs and his voice was getting further and further away. He grinned about something I hadn't heard, and on his lips the image flashed again. *No. No. No.*

We turned onto the Strand into the stream of shoppers and the thoughts opened out, blossomed, swallowed every person in London. Now everyone was naked and prostrate on the pavement, every man and woman performing in the mass orgy that had writhed in my mind for a decade. Even *things* became sex – the Vaudeville's curved arch and the Savoy's deep V – they twisted into obscenities in my vision and engulfed all that was lovely. The sunset burning the old bricks red. The music from the gilded lobbies – all were lost in rolling folds of flesh. I was no longer in London on a hot, hot day in July, I was inside my head, where I'd been for half of my life, pacing the same old strip of earth bare.

It doesn't usually stop for hours or days or years, but something Erik said just then cut through; with a single sentence spoken in his deep, lilting voice, I was there again in London, with the the candy-coloured lanterns and the waterspray rainbows, a part of now:

'So if you're up for it, Rose, I'd love you to come on the trip and be my writer.'

When Doves Cry

I walked onto my Shoreditch estate and saw the two fat women that were always sat smoking outside the launderette. One of them was laughing so hard she was spilling tea all over her vast Fruit of the Loom T-shirt and the other was red-faced from coughing. They raised their mugs to cheers me as I passed, their gelatinous bodies wobbling with waves of suppressed giggles. Usually all I saw were their stretch-marked tera-tits and worse, all purple and veiny and folding over the plastic chairs and towards me. But this time I waved back, smiling. Really smiling this time.

I stepped into my hallway and listened for sounds of my flatmates but there were none, so I skipped to my bedroom and squealed and did a little run on the spot. I put on 'When Doves Cry' and sat down and stood up and sat down again and hugged myself. I looked at myself wide-eyed in the mirror and grinned and swore.

With one too-enthusiastic hip thrust I slipped on the laminate, clattered into the wall, and erupted into a fit of nervous gigs, then catwalked back across the room singing the lyrics loud, 'THIS IS WHAT IT SOUNDS LIKE WHEN DOVES CRY'. Soon I was pulling my knickers into my bum crack and doing the Beyoncé booty shake in the mirror, because everyone knows that when doves cry they sound like the clacking cheeks of an untoned arse.

I made a rare effort to make my bed and smoothed out the creases until it looked lovely, then I lay on my front on the cotton and swayed my legs from the knee, picking at the duvet's lace ruff. Minutes turned into hours as I imagined in great detail the leaving party and the beaches and me: tanned, confident and happy, and my now-toned arse, resplendent in the tropical sun.

This was happening to *me*: Rose Bretécher, aged 24, from Dudley. I'd be travelling the world, expenses paid, fulfilling a youthful dream, romantic as youth itself; seeing new, strange faces every morning, watching new, strange sunsets every night. I would savour the skies more than anything; more than anything the skies would move me. I would swallow the stars.

But what eluded me that night – and that night alone, because when I awoke the next day the euphoria had ebbed away into fear – was that the whole trip could well be irrelevant. For that night alone I'd forgotten that I was ill; forgotten that this once-in-a-lifetime experience might just skim the surface, and that my secret condition might render the sensually-rich leagues between London and Sydney as unreal as Avalon.

Many more times I would meet Erik to talk about the trip and many more times he would enthuse about this phenomenal project he'd brought into being. But each time he traced our journey with his finger between the salt cellars, painting pictures of Middle Eastern ruins and Nepalese panoramas, the sex thoughts with their keen barbs stabbed on, and I wasn't really listening to him, and I wasn't really there.

Pop Will Eat Itself

No-one could have guessed that something was going to explode inside me. I was a happy child.

I was the youngest of four kids in a big, Catholic family, and there was always dressing-up and water-fights and conkering and Captain Haddock; orphaned pigeons to break our hearts over and trips to pat the pigs down Pig's Lane. I remember the electric hush when we saw a wild deer in the Wyre Forest, and the low buzz of Dad's voice through his back when he carried me, even though I was a bit too big to be carried. I remember Mom's hand reaching from the front seat to stroke the chubby little knee behind her. How she'd rearrange my saggy socks without looking.

I remember the thrill of naughtiness when my parents' backs were turned – the daily acts of gleeful perversion: mixing cat poo poison in jam jars; singing Gregorian chants over dead mice in the garden; pulling faces at Father John at the 'Body of Christ' bit.

And I remember the bums – me and my older brother Patty were positively *enraptured* by bums. We made sourdough bums; we drew bums on frosted windows; we painted faces on our bums and made sumo bums with our swimming trunks. On rainy afternoons we'd huddle under the bed with the neighbours' kids and sniff each other's fingers after a diligent bum-scratch, adopting the mannerisms of the most sincere sommeliers and applauding the hints and top notes. It became a game. We called it Smell Bums.

Our biggest brother Ted knew very well that he could elicit shrieks of delight from his younger siblings by mooning out of a bedroom window on Easter morning, or spelling 'ARSE' on the scrabble board, or farting during mealtimes. How we'd *roll* with laughter at Dad's disgruntled face and booming reprimands: 'You're a DRAAAIN, Ted, a shameless vulgarian'.

And if the dog farted–well–there really was nothing better. Me and Patty would be finished, irretrievable, *howling*. Dad would look into his plate, eyebrows raised, quietly building his next forkful and rueing the hopeless inefficacy of his stoic politeness in the face of his own baying brood. We'd be falling off our chairs, peas flying everywhere, food unswallowed in our wide, laughing mouths.

No-one could have guessed.

We lived in an old Black Country market town. Granddad had worked in the steelworks for forty years on the banks of the river, when the water was black and the town was prospering, and there hadn't been a bargain greeting card shop or a Kwik Save to be seen. By the early 1990s the council was trying to spruce up the town by putting mosaics in the subway and bright yellow benches in the bus station, but they'd taken out its clanging heart and they couldn't stop it dying.

We lived in a 1950s semi behind the train station, and you could hear the platform announcements clearly from the garden. Patty used to climb the lime tree by the back fence and belt out erroneous timetable information and made-up destinations through a traffic cone. I'd stand at the bottom of the trunk, jumping up and down, screaming laughing.

Me and Patty were separated from Ted and our older sister Maggie by eight long years, and they were therefore our benchmarks of being – our *heroes*. We listened to their alien lives develop through the walls – Guns N' Roses and Pop Will Eat Itself and Nirvana – and when they let us sit on their beds and spray their deodorants and build castles with their cassette collections, we were kings.

Back then Ted and Maggie were both devoted Rockers, and all their friends had long hair and chokers and big T-shirts. In the Black Country you were either a Rocker or a Townie, they told me. Townie boys were called Kevs and they had curtained hair and stud earrings and collared shirts. Townie girls were called Sharons and they wore hair mousse and lip liner and plastic miniskirts. *I* was going to be a Rocker when *I* grew up, I knew that for sure. When I was seven years old I chose a pair of imitation Doc Martens for my school shoes and Ted said they were 'wicked, man'. I was high for weeks. Twenty years later he would cry as he hugged his little sister – as tall as him now and a howling Sharon – sorry he never knew.

Late Night Love

Baron Hieronymus Karl Friedrich von Münchhausen was a teller of tall tales. A German nobleman in the 18th century who served in the military, he was renowned for recounting outrageously farfetched stories about his adventures. He once claimed to have pulled himself *and* his horse out of a swamp, using only his *hair* as a rope. Like a boss.

Today, the baron's gift for flagrant fabrication lives on in medical nomenclature. Munchausen's Syndrome, or factitious disorder, is a psychological and behavioural condition where, for complex psychiatric reasons, a person seeks attention and sympathy by pretending to be ill or by inducing symptoms of illness in themselves.

I'd venture that as kids, most of us knew the tricks of a good sickie – sometimes the lure of *GMTV* and *Bargain Hunt* and Frosties-for-lunch was simply too great, and we had *no* choice but to conjure our best Tiny Tim chest-rattle. But Munchausen's is in another realm entirely, and in extreme cases, people will undergo invasive surgery or rub dirt into open wounds to make the ruse more convincing.

I don't know why the lying started. Things were normal and good.

I went to school and to Brownies and to swimming lessons. Every weekend I played busily with my little friends

– hopscotch and curby and Barbies. We used to call Barbie and Ken Fanny and Dick and make them make babies in a shoebox together. We used to play Kiss The Bride, reenacting *Neighbours* weddings, pressing our faces together and giggling at the imaginary priest's bidding. We made talcum-powder cigarettes and fairy cakes and friendship bracelets. We giggled at the great, bursting nummies of the breast-feeding women outside nursery.

At home my parents were full of the expressions of love: back scratches in bed every morning, and praise in all the right places, and hugs and kisses all through the days. And any hardship they hid from me – mental illness and physical illness and benefits – because as the baby I was protected from the enormity of these things. I was kept safe and happy and oblivious.

So I can't say why I started faking asthma attacks when I was eight years old. I'd take these massive gulps of air and deliberately hyperventilate until I was dizzy, commanding the concern of my buddies and commandeering the play-ground for myself. Finding my lies rewarded with love, I'd be rushed by a fawning dinner lady to the potpourri-smelling reception area with the offices all around and the beige seats, where there were no other kids and it was quiet. She'd always get me a paper bag to breathe into, so I'd do what I'd seen on *Casualty*, and make the bag go big and small and then big again. Sometimes they'd let me go home and Mom would give me warm Ribena, like she gave the dog when the dog got spayed – I remember the puppy pencil tail beating feebly on the lino.

Nor can I say why I pretended to faint on a school trip when I was 10. We were at a butterfly farm and it was really hot in there, and my best friend fainted and got embosomed by a jolly teacher, so I figured I'd give it a go, too. I wanted some of that nuzzling action.

And I certainly don't know why I skived pretty much my entire first year of high school when I was 11 going on 12. It's true that initially I had a mild case of mastoiditis (like sinusitis, affecting the mastoid bones behind the ear), but over the course of 160 absent schooldays – 160 little red strokes in the register, the teachers tut-tutting each time – I vastly exaggerated the symptoms and the pain, groaning over headaches that weren't there, groaning myself all the way to hospitalisation, a stay on a children's ward, and to a CAT scan in a private clinic that my parents couldn't afford.

It was a layered, 24/7 performance: every night when Mom and Dad had tucked me up, I'd keep myself awake listening to the *Titanic* soundtrack and BRMB Radio's Late Night Love on my Walkman. Then, when enough time had passed so I could realistically have slept and awoken again – usually a couple of hours – I'd cry out as though I was in pain, until one of my parents got out of bed and cooed me back to sleep. Mom would whisper to me in French as she stroked my hair, calling me *lapin* and *bichette* and telling me not to worry: '*Ne t'inquiète pas chérie*'. I guess I unknowingly became addicted to the affirmation, because for seven months I couldn't sleep without that midnight cuddle from someone who loved me.

I was barely conscious of my burgeoning worries, but the following year, when I was 13, I began to record them in a diary – a little WH Smith jotter with a modest title scrawled on the red cover in Tippex: *The Vale of Soul Making*. I must have picked up on the phrase in RE lessons or on *The Simpsons* – a Keatsian conceptualisation of the world as a vast valley of trials and tribulations in which we must become complete. Our Souls are not made until they 'acquire identities', Keats said, 'till each one is personally itself'.

Apart from the lyrics of Charlene's 'I've Never Been To Me' ('I've been to paradise but I've never been to me') and that quote about 'if you love someone set them free . . .', which I'd seen in a butterfly photo frame in Clinton's Cards, this was the most mind-blowingly profound thing I'd ever heard.

What does it mean to be 'personally yourself'? How do you 'acquire' an identity? This diary, this *tome*, *The Vale of Soul Making*, would chart my finding out – it would document my journey of discovery, my forging of a pure identity. On 10th November 1999 I wrote the first entry:

'I guessed now was a good time to begin this diary (I prefer to call it an epic life story) as we are nearing the millennium. From now till the millennium I shall try to inform you as often as possible about the changing world around me. This will hopefully include:

- My thoughts on heavy subjects
- Lads (my fancies, etc.)
- Friends and family
- Christmas
- Current world events
- My dog
- God – views, queries
- Homework, school, etc.

I suppose I am pretty lucky, not everyone gets to see a millennium. Yet through all the hype and excitement, I am not too sure about it. There are things I don't understand and I worry about them. I worry that the world will end or a nuclear war will start or technology will grow out of control. I must admit to myself, I am a worrier. If it's not a German test it's nuclear warfare, there is always something playing on my mind. I worry about a comet hitting the earth, destroying all life as we know it, like how the dinosaurs died out. I really need to organise a millennium party else I run the risk of spending it at the Parish Centre.'

The millennium passed without incident, and my two equal concerns of global holocaust and spending New Year's Eve in the church hall with my parents were proved unfounded. I ended up going to a party with a school friend and her folks, wearing jelly shoes over gold sparkly tights, and the purple velvet Tammy Girl dress I'd bought especially. We drank Dr Pepper and danced to Robbie Williams until 12.30am!!!

But the year 2000 was monumental for other reasons. I was 14 now and I was starting to remember how many lies I'd told when I was younger. Now I was more aware of my parents' adult world, I was able to imagine them, exhausted and frayed, getting up in the middle of the night in the middle of winter to tend to the crocodile tears of their youngest daughter. The *worry* I must have caused. They'd given me a *brain scan,* for fuck's sake, because the *mastoiditis* was so near the brain they 'didn't want to take any chances'.

*

My betrayal had been watertight. My deception complete. The immensity dawned on me. Asthma attacks, skiving, my secret nighttime world of lies: these were unforgiveable, and bad things would happen because I had transgressed.

The guilt was tinder on the pile.

After Shocks

I met my first boyfriend Greg in the park when I was 14 going on 15. He was playing keepy-uppy with his friends and I was making daisy chains with mine. Someone got dared into talking to them, and soon we started meeting each other after school and going to the Banks' pub round the corner, where the boys used to send us to the bar with puffed-out chests to buy Bacardi Breezers and After Shocks.

Greg and I started holding hands and going round to each other's houses for tea, and, as *The Vale of Soul Making* chronicles, sending each other texts of noteworthy romance: 'Hi hows it going? wot u up 2 coz im meant 2 b revisin but I cant be arsed. can I have ur home num coz I'll give u a call? laterz, lotsa luv.' Your weekly £5 top-up had to go a long way in those days, and economy of language always trumped mystique.

Cut to the giddy wow of my first kiss outside Greg's parents' house two weeks later. Orange streetlights. Cars rolling over gravel in the distance. *Corrie* blaring behind a hundred curtained windows.

I'd been aware of sexual feelings for a few years. Indiscriminate, omnivorous, generous feelings, which could be roused by the slightest hint of rudeness: a long-anticipated snog on *Baywatch*; a sliver of sideboob on *Wish You Were Here*; a whispered 'condoms' on *Grange Hill*.

I knew that *boys* felt like this and that Adrian Mole felt like this, but not girls. Somehow I sensed that the feelings in my little girl's body were not normal, and every default joke about the masturbatory habits of teenage boys confirmed my hunch. Even the teachers were in on it: the down-with-the-kids teachers with their rib-poking wise cracks about boys getting distracted from their homework. Never a mention of girls. Girls never got a nod nod wink wink or a nudge in the ribs, even though we could distract ourselves as enthusiastically as any strapping young man. And I still remember the hot-faced embarrassment of biology class, feeling like I was the only girl in my 1000-strong school who was fascinated by nakedness.

But now: my first kiss, the swoons of all of Hollywood happening right here. And then, over the next few weeks, the singular, never-again, star-defying optimism of first love. The childlike let's-stay-together-forevers, the you're-my-soul-mates, the you're-my-first-my-last-my-everythings. The preposterous but so-real sincerity. All of the anxieties of my life seeming to melt away.

And then, as the months passed, growing more used to the feeling of my boyfriend's body so close to mine, I started to remember other, smaller bodies that'd once been just as close. A slow-dawning comprehension as grainy pictures from years past presented themselves and I slowly began to realise: sex had been a part of my life since I was a small child, aped on Sunday afternoons with tiny, giggling school-boys and girls. Fanny and Dick and Kiss The Bride and the beloved Smell Bums. Now my mind was opened, just a sliver, but it was enough: consciousness sucked into my head at a thousand miles per hour and sent shrapnel and sex whirling and whirling in miles-wide circles under my skull, because for years and years, on Babar bed sheets and at the backs of gardens, I'd done terrible, sinful things.

Catastrophe was coming.

Boiled Potatoes

The image flickered in my mind for the first time. I put down my cutlery and pushed a boiled potato around in the buttery droplets on my plate. Dad sat across from me, ten thousand miles away, and Mom was hunting draughts at the window. On the stone kitchen tiles the dog sat bored and sceptical, eyebrow dots twitching.

My throat was closing over.

Stoned and smiling, Patty sat next to me, resting his elbows on teenage knees too high for the table. He bit his lip and looked sidelong at Mom and Dad to check they weren't watching as he teased the dog with a tiny piece of meat, bringing it close to the misty whiskers and quivering nose. She patted a furry paw on his leg and let out a little squeak, and he looked at me for my surefire grin of complicity.

I knew it was funny. It was definitely funny. But the giggles didn't come, this time.

The fleshy image flickered again as he popped the lid of the ketchup bottle in and out, again and again, before shaking it and pouring a lake onto his plate. I picked some mashed broccoli seeds from the tablecloth as the image flashed brighter and my ribcage tightened – giant insect legs squeezing me for the first time. I rose, not looking at anyone, and said 'thank you for the meal' in the routine lilt. The dog danced around my feet as I reached for the kitchen cupboard where we kept the leash.

The street was dark and cold and the dog strained against the collar, stiffening now and then at the sight of a cat. Someone was burning bracken somewhere and the air was mossy. In the wood I couldn't see my feet, just two iridescent eyes flashing between the trees.

I turned the topsoil of my mind for an answer about what the image might have meant, but the possibilities made me dizzy, and I had to sit on a wall. It was waxy with lime leaves and snail silver. Beyond the trees, the noise of distant traffic was the noise of everyone else, everywhere, and it frightened me in a dull, shapeless way, with the intangible threat of a half-remembered dream. The dog's breath was catching the white of an old street lamp a little way off.

The more I tried to stop thinking about the image – a little boy naked – the quicker it flickered. It flickered and flickered and flickered, and something like lint was invading my lungs. I pulled my thighs up to my chest and felt my cheeks flush hot as I pressed my eye sockets against my knees, breathing hard. When the dog licked my ankle I raised my head and gasped as if breaking from water. Fuzzy green circles trembled in my vision for a couple of seconds before twirling off left and right, and then a stillness came over me.

I mouthed the words slowly to the dark, slamming my hands against my mouth, 'What if I'm a paedo—?'

And with that question I was sucked inside my head, where I spent the next decade fretting at the unanswerable like a fly on a lamp; all the while telling no-one, all the while playing a role in life – a role to belie my secret. All the while being everything that I thought a teenage girl should be: fun, flirtatious and hungry for adventure.

Return Of The Mack

We'd been up all night and my eyes were sore. Hackney's drunks had long since knocked themselves out and the street was quiet save for the loud-silent swoosh of Toby's cheek against my ear. We held hands in the half light as we waited.

When we'd fallen in love we already knew I'd be leaving. We'd always been holding our breath and waiting for the stillness, for the exhale, for the time when I wasn't about to leave and do the riskiest thing I'd ever done. Now the moment was here and I was speeding 10,000 miles away from him, carrying a decade's worth of unspeakable thoughts.

Looking up at him and wringing his sleeve, I opened my mouth to tell him my secret. But how could I say the words? Inside my head they were private and only-mine, and if they got out I wouldn't be able to control them, or control what they did to our relationship. *They'll ruin it*, I thought, as I pressed my face into his coat, saying nothing.

From here the warehouse across the street looked black against the dawn sky, and it was uncharacteristically silent. Usually the murmur of minimal techno could be heard all through the day and night, or the occasional thump of cult 90s R&B – the Mack returned twice a week, at least.

From Toby's balcony you could see right into the warehouse apartments, and we'd often stood gaping at their inhabitants' achingly curated retro wares. Once I yanked

Toby's jeans and boxers down to his ankles and we couldn't breathe for laughing as he scrambled to pull them up. I hope the guys across the street saw: *THAT'S what I think of your Marshall-amp-coffee-table and your Britvic pineapple and your David Lynch poster and your gold bust of Lionel Richie.* It's probably safe to say that they peered through *our* windows with similar scepticism, too, because all young Hackney immigrants are wont to believe that *their* collection of clutter is born of genuine passion, of a superior fondness for ThunderCats or Babycham or Hi-Tec or Hall & Oates, unlike everyone else's tastes, which are contrived and homogeneous and not-to-be-trusted. But hiding under the surface layers of tie dye and stonewash denim is an endemic self-consciousness: niggling little doubts about originality which flicker threateningly at the edge of coolness. They were probably looking across the street and asking themselves the same question that everyone around here was secretly asking of everyone else, yet never daring to utter: 'are we *them*?'

Yes. Yes you are.

When the taxi arrived Toby and I said goodbye, kissing long on the lips as the engine whirred.

'You're going to see so many amazing things,' he said, holding my face with both hands.

No-one knows the things I see, I nodded.

'The time'll go quick, love.'

Every minute feels like an hour, I thought, smiling.

'I'll see you in Goa halfway through. We'll drink some cocktails and see some wazzy animals. It's gonna be brilliant.'

I love you so much, I thought. 'I love you so much,' I said.

*

As the car moved off I watched him fade into the distance and wave little waves, and as the car turned at the end of the road I just glimpsed the red bobble of his hat flop forwards as he bowed his head. He'd put that hat on with childlike pride the day he bought it, I remember – the pavement had glistened with frost. I cooed over him uncontrollably whenever he wore anything woollen.

I looked at my lap and thought about how long it would be before I saw him again: Goa seemed like *years* away. I picked at my cuticles, working dry skin shreds away from the pink flesh of my thumbs. I thought about us kissing in our big coats and his wet face in the orange streetlight, and how he'd shouldered my bag heavily down the stairs, big as a pig with four months of my life inside.

Through the faggy air the taxi drove down an empty Mare Street, past takeaway owners sweeping chips from the pavement, and a couple of stragglers stumbling from the steaming doors of The Dolphin. The plaintive thump of their swan song – David Guetta or Calvin Harris or Swedish House Mafia or something similar – could just be heard from inside.

I found a piece of grit on the taxi seat and pressed it into my palm, making little pink indents in my skin, all in a line. Shoreditch, Kings Cross and Marylebone twinkled past in the morning traffic.

Since the moonlit night in the wood with the dog, I'd lived 3,830 days of graphic, wall-to-wall thoughts, and told no-one – and now I had 118 days ahead of me, in a bus full of strangers. How the hell was I going to pull this off? How the hell was I going to make myself better? How the *hell* was

I going to save my relationship? *I don't know. I don't know. I don't know.* I had to try harder than ever. I had reach deep inside myself and find New Rose. She had to be in there somewhere.

Demolition Tits

At 7am the taxi arrived at a car park in West London, where I met the rest of my travel buddies – and within five minutes I'd seen everyone butt naked in piercing, cold-light detail. My thumbs bled inside my coat pockets.

Particularly sticky that morning were one of the crew members' tits, which swung like wrecking balls through my mind for a good two minutes as she chatted to me about what she'd packed. On she talked as her tits swung repeatedly into my vision, and my throat tightened more and more. *It means nothing*, I said inside my head. When another crew member (the one whose bollockskin had stretched out before me like a pelt rug when he'd first shook my hand) interrupted her with a question, I was relieved to no longer be engaged in conversation, and separated myself from the group slightly, so as not to invite any more chitchat and subsequent lacerating visuals.

I imagined myself speeding back to Toby's in a taxi and shaking my head against his chest and sobbing, 'I can't do it I can't do it I can't do it', my cheeks flushed rosy, my tears quivering dramatically in my eyes. But no. I had to make myself better – I had to come back to him in four months, a changed person.

Tomorrow we'd be making our first stop of the trip at Oktoberfest – a Munich beer festival to which booze tourists from around the world flocked with the sole desire to get smashed out of their faces and ogle the pushed-up mammaries of myriad dirndled fraus. Already in that cold car park there were whispers of excitement among the crew, which intensified my foreboding. Festivals spun me out like nothing else.

My mind had already spent *hours* scoping out the imagined crowd, trying to anticipate how it'd make me feel. The sheer number of triggers was naturally a problem – if imagining one person naked was unpleasant, imagining 50,000 people naked was downright grim. But more problematic was the pressure, on such occasions, to have a superlatively good time, to have 'a day to remember'. I felt this great sense of 'supposed to' prodding at me, as I did on all momentous occasions. You're *supposed* to feel euphoric at pool parties and on camping trips and on the beach: these are the landmarks of a successful youth. But in my experience, 'supposed to' kind of kills the experience before it's even started. It totally precludes any chance of serendipity.

Everyone looked tired, having undoubtedly spent the last few nights mulling over the finer details of travelling 10,000 miles shoulder-to-shoulder with people they barely knew. But we soon switched to japester mode to pose for a jazz-hands photo – a photo which would reach Facebook within minutes, telling an untrue story of carefree, unbridled youth. Because nervousness must not be admitted in the face of Fun.

We each hauled our bags onto the bus and chose a bunk on the top deck before regrouping round the downstairs tables, and by 8am we'd started driving, due in Dover in a couple of hours. Everyone chatted politely and tentatively, exchanging tales about full moon parties and Inca trails, and I sat among them, smiling daftly, trying not to let on that bellends were invading the scene from every angle and slapping against the lips of whoever was speaking.

I scanned my body in search of the arousal sensations which so often accompanied such visual spectacles, then tensed up my muscles when I thought I felt a twinge. The more I tried to block it out, the more intense it became.

The crew had their own stories to tell, of course. They'd all had tearful goodbyes with their own loved ones that morning, but it didn't matter because they weren't people to me. Right now they were just fleshy satellites, orbiting me as I sat rigid and ridiculous on that dusty seat, distinguishable only by what imagery they provoked, and the ruthlessness with which their anatomical details burnt themselves onto my retinas.

I'd already decided that they weren't going to know me. If I couldn't even tell my own boyfriend my secret, how was I going to tell anyone here? Drop it into a conversation about *The Beach* or *Mr Nice*? I didn't think it'd go down too well. I got the feeling that Travelling only accommodated neuroses if they were stylised in indie films with hallucinogenics and bikini-clad girls. Anything else would be a drag, and not befitting this once-in-a-lifetime experience. 'Look where you are. Look at the *ocean*,' I imagined them saying when I confessed my distress. No. I couldn't do it. Of our travels we only publish the smiles and the sunsets, censoring sadness. It just doesn't look good on Instagram.

Soon weariness triumphed and everyone found little corners of the bus in which to listen to music or read.

I stayed where I was, facing backwards and watching the bus chug out its endless gossamer of grey, thinking about the tits and hilts with whom I was about to cross the globe, and about the impending festival of sex which loomed darker in my imagination with every mile we drove.

Where will I run?

How will I hide the thoughts?

Beep. A text from Toby telling me to check my bag. Breathless, I stumbled up the mountain of strangers' shoes which had amassed on the bus stairs, and started pulling out tight folds of clothes from my rucksack. Rolled in one of my jumpers I found the teddy bear he'd had since he was born, and I let out a tiny squeal as I pressed him against my chest, resting my chin on his head. Already I missed Toby with a burn in my chest – that pre-language fire which tells our bodies when something essential is missing.

With my thumb I found the threadbare patch below the bear's ear, the scuffed nose and the flattened muzzle. I could tell *this* guy my secrets, no probs. I could curl up with him at night and tell him the whole damn lot, right from the start, like I used to tell my teddies stories when I was young: 'Once upon time in a land called Dudley, long, long ago, lived a little girl called Rose. One night, in a moonlit wood, she came face to face with a giant monster which had been sleeping underground for many years. Terrified, she tried to run away, but the faster she ran, the quicker the monster chased her—'

—'It's going to be fucking amazing,' someone said at the far end of the bus. I recognised the voice of Demolition Tits and the girl whose tongue I'd imagined sucking when she'd kissed me on each cheek, plus that of a boy whose name I hadn't yet learned. They were talking about Oktoberfest's so-called Pig Pen – a gated-off area of the festival full of horny, pissed-up blokes, who waited to rip off the bra of any unsuspecting woman who entered. I visualised it and twitched. 'Everything's fair game in the Pig Pen,' the boy's voice said, laughing.

I lay on my bed, pretending to read. I kneaded the mattress with my hand, causing nebulous, grey dust to plume against the black mouth of my sleeping bag.

I'm supposed to be excited.

I'm supposed to be excited.

I'm supposed to be excited.

We drove into Munich the following afternoon. In the suburbs there were concrete houses with square windows arranged uniformly across their frontages. Giant cylindrical structures towered above the skyline, a hundred metres high, fulfilling some unknown function above the city. It was a bright, blue day and the clouds themselves became cunts in my eyes.

Kickers Or Pods

Who am I? Who am I? Who am I? Who was this person who could think such a terrible thing? The terror of suddenly not knowing the meaning of my thoughts, of suddenly not recognising the voice inside my head which had been Me since Me was made. The terror of doubting your You-ness. Where is You? Where does it live and how do you find it when it's gone? How does a 15-year-old girl get through each suburban school day when she thinks she's a paedophile?

Last night my life had changed forever. In the morning I woke up to a feeling of orchestral doom, an unending crescendo of stabbing staccato trills. *Am I a paedophile? Am I a paedophile? Am I a paedophile?* I'd hoped the night's sleep would break the tension, but the thoughts seemed even worse now, and still the strings rose and rose.

On the bus to school the usual jostle and smell of Lynx and Cheetos. The windows opaque and sweaty, save for the odd bit of bubble-writing: 'Sam is fridge' and 'Dan 4 Buffy 4eva. I.D.S.T'.

If Destroyed Still True.

A morning text to Greg: 'Hi baby. Av a good day. Cu in twn l8r. Lv u', typed by guilty fingers.

With my friends I talked and smiled and nodded: a top

layer of function, and one layer down a barrage of thoughts and doubts and questions. Not Kickers-or-Pods questions or Keanu-or-Leo questions. Terrible, secret questions.

Did I commit paedophilia when I was a kid?

Will I ever do it again?

Will the children remember what I did and tell the police?

Will I get taken away from my family and locked up?

Will my picture be in the paper?

How could I have done those things?

And the attempt at answers.

No.

No.

No.

It disgusts me.

I'd rather die.

I could never.

I would never.

I have never.

And all this somehow happening at the same time as my mouth was talking, all the thoughts piling on top of each other just behind my eyes where my Me used to be.

On the way to first lesson – physics – a group of older lads had made a human gauntlet for anyone trying to get into the science corridor, and they were wolf-whistling every girl who walked through them. One pinched my bum and I was embarrassed and angry but my words came out all wrong, and instead of saying 'piss off' or 'fuck you' I mumbled 'piss you!' and they laughed and crowed 'piss you' after me as I shuffled blushing into the science block, tugging on my too-long skirt.

By lunchtime the doubts were incessant and I was trying to dispel them by dissecting my memory for clues about my identity. As I sat on a windy bench, chatting with friends and eating my packed lunch (ham and marge sarnie: standard), I was silently interrogating every pretend kiss and cuddle I'd had at sleepovers as a child; every hairless knob I'd etched with compasses into waxy table tops; every *Sugar* magazine I'd read by torchlight with complicit little classmates. Memories coming back now of an eight-year-old me and two classmates, giddy like sprites over the thought of an imagined 'sextaurant' where love-hungry customers came to buy kisses from waiters. Of *Saved By The Bell – The Uni Years*: a game in which in our much-abused teddy bears were behoved to dramatise Zack and Kelly's long-awaited consummation. And of—

—*oh no*— I nearly choked on my Capri Sun—

—of *100.7 Fart FM*: mine and Patty's amateur radio show for which we'd blasted trumps into a Fisher-Price cassette recorder and edited them into weekly hit parades, summarising each effort with Mark Goodier-gusto (Celine Dion's 'My Fart Will Go On' had been number one for 16 weeks).

All these delectable, filthy sparkles of a child's boundless imagination were twisted into something threatening, because they all seemed to support my new fears about my capacity for depravity. *How could I have been so perverted?*

Nauseous, I ate my daily Aero and went back to lessons. Two more hours of lessons that afternoon. Five more tomorrow. And the day after, and every day, and all that year, and all the year after that. By the time I sat my GCSEs 11,000 hours later, the images and doubts were flashing up like searchlights in my face, 24/7, and during long exams, every second stroke of my pen marked the flicker of forbidden obscenities in my brain. Sometimes I got up in the night and had five seconds of forgetfulness, but by the time I'd stepped blinking into the bathroom's tungsten light, I'd always remembered – the thoughts had always caught up. And the next day there'd be teeth marks in the toilet roll where I'd stopped myself from screaming. *Who am I? Who am I? Who am I?*

Every week at church I saw this one old guy at the front of the Communion queue, and since we were tiny kids Patty and I had called him The Cod because of his singularly bulbous eyes, and his lips which sucked and roamed for the wafer in the priest's fingers. Every time he walked past our pew, my brother and I would guppy at each other and puff out our faces, spluttering into our cupped hands to shield our laughter from Dad. 'Thanks be to Cod', 'The Lord Our Cod', 'Cod the Father', we'd snigger. The ultimate triumph was eliciting giggles from Mom, and getting her to laugh became a weekly game. But after the thoughts started the game just stopped. I knew it was funny. It was definitely funny. But I couldn't laugh honestly anymore, because the would-be giggles always had to rise through the funk of explicit, illicit child pornography, and by the time they got to the surface, they were weak and shaken and not real.

And then there was the Penitential Rite, the Confession and Absolution. Mea culpa. My fault.
I confess to almighty God
and to you, my brothers and sisters,
that I have greatly sinned,

in my thoughts and in my words,
in what I have done and in what I have failed to do,
through my fault, through my own fault,
through my own most grievous fault;
therefore I ask blessed Mary ever-Virgin,
all the Angels and Saints,
and you, my brothers and sisters,
to pray for me to the Lord our God.
Amen

There it was. I was at fault because God had said so. Barbie and Ken had been my fault, Kiss The Bride had been my fault, Smell Bums had been fault. My thoughts, even, my unstoppable thoughts – they too were my fault. And I'd lie in bed on Sunday nights murmuring that line over and over: 'I have greatly sinned in my thoughts. I have greatly sinned in my thoughts. I have greatly sinned in my thoughts', and I'd slip into sleep on the damp pillow, trying to focus on the sound of my parents' heavy sleepbreathing in the next room, or on the ceiling's fluorescent stars above me: collected from cereal boxes over years and years, the last glows of a Me which now seemed dimmed forever.

Egg Monkey

From the brow of the hill I looked down on the 100-acre site of Oktoberfest, where giant inflatable beer steins and fiber-glass Bavarians dominated the rollercoaster horizon. Already, costumed festival-goers were streaming past us back to the campsites, all battered and swaying and smelling sour.

Every time someone's flesh brushed against mine, a fair-ground hammer fell on my throat, sending a weight rushing down into me, lighting the cavities of my chest with trills of anxiety. Six million people visit Oktoberfest every year, and every one of them was swimming in the pink-blackness between each blink of my eyes.

It means nothing, I told myself.

We herded down the hill and through the gates towards the giant Ferris wheel, stopping just short because someone was puking from a carriage about halfway up and blasting their dinner all over the tarmac. A girl screamed as the splat sent flecks of vomit up her legs.

Against the side of a fast food van a sweaty man was sneaking the hand of some obese stranger down his trousers and kissing her chin with bovine relish.

I darted after the rest of the group, looking at the ground, and whenever I peeped up to check I hadn't lost the back of their heads, a cleavage or suede-clad crotch scorched my sight and I flinched my eyes back down to the ground, where ticker tape and discarded burgers rushed past on the grey. Red, blue and pink neons reflected in smashed glasses, dizzying me, and the sickly-sweet smell of candy floss and browned onions made me feel pickled inside. Everywhere I saw faces awestruck by the fairground lights and flamboyant costumes. 'I'm supposed to be excited,' I whispered.

We stopped outside one of the huge beer tents. Opposite its massive doors there was a 50-metre-long grassy bank on which people were passed out or fighting. Men pissed and puked in the bushes while paramedics carried ambulance stretchers past. Right there, about halfway up the bank, a middle aged woman lifted up her skirts in front of hundreds of passers-by and squatted for a piss. The crew groaned. I jerked my head away and crossed my legs and squeezed tight to block out the inevitable arousal.

Torrent over, a headcount confirmed that we'd all made it through the fray, and we went into the tent en masse. Garlands and streamers hung from the apex of the huge hall and festooned the elevated bandstand, beneath which thousands of drinkers in traditional dress occupied rows of benches as far as you could see. The crew stood agape, thoroughly wowed, and one of the girls grabbed my hand in excitement. I squeezed my legs together again, almost shaking now.

While the others ogled our surrounds, I scanned the huge room for evidence of the Pig Pen. I wanted to find out where it was so I could avoid it if I needed to – I didn't react well to surprises.

Weeks later I'd hear other crew members say that those first few Oktoberfest moments were some of the most exciting of the trip. They'd describe the rush, the heady atmosphere and the thrill of the music. But I didn't feel those things because my head was still in the crowd outside; or on the bank trying to figure out how that pissy woman had made me feel; or in the moonlit wood, all those years ago. Hypervigilant, I was everywhere but here, noticing every detail but feeling nothing.

We chose a spot and sat on a bench next to a group of podgy Englishmen wearing blue, personalised football shirts. Each shirt had the number '69' printed on the back and a respective nickname. 'Egg Monkey' and 'Beer Monster' were in particularly high spirits, standing on the table and entreating passing women to get their tits out.

Along the aisles, German boys in felt hats carried baskets of brezn and knödel, and ancient, leather-faced beer wenches barrelled along, six full beer steins in each arm. Erik hailed one down and planted a comedy kiss on her puckered mouth, shouting 'thanks, babes' as she thrust the drinks into our hands. I sipped my beer like a deer at a watering hole.

The group cheered and wolf-whistled to see an old man wearing nothing but Italian flag Y-fronts with the image of Michaelangelo's David's penis embroidered into the crotch, his chest hair matted with spilt beer. A buxom German girl was trying to take his photo but her eyes were moving in different directions and she forgot what she was doing before she got around to pressing the shutter, leaving the crestfallen stallion doing a 'which way to the beach?' muscle flex, alone. But the urge to laugh was trampled by the urge to run, so I excused myself with smiles and left the group and headed for the bathroom queue, where a spindly young man in Bavarian dress was stalking the line and taking high-angled shots down the drunkest girls' dresses with a camera concealed in his palm. I jumped the line, slammed a cubicle door behind me and held my head in my hands. My stomach turned to surround-sound retching.

I thought, for a moment, when the floor-shadow of the girl in the next cubicle had me crossing my legs tight to stave off a fatty, that the worst of the anxiety was on its way, but by breathing deep and telling myself that the tingling feeling *meant nothing, meant nothing, meant nothing, meant nothing, meant nothing*, I was able to calm down and reapply my make-up.

As I gulped my second drink back in the hall, Ein Prosit, a traditional beer hall song, started up from the bandstand, and the whole crowd rose as one onto the benches to sing along. We clunked our steins together again and put our arms around each other. I looked into the middle of the huddle to see everyone naked from the waist down, Winnie-the-Pooh style, and the question 'who would I like to give head to most?' buzzed at the front of my mind. I closed my eyes and tried to ignore it but it loudened by the second. I had no choice, I didn't want to, but my brain was already doing it: looking down into the naked scrum and imagine each sweaty crotch in vivid detail.

A smartphone flashed in my face and I hid behind my thick stein as much as possible, because the tapping and sliding of fingers against those greasy screens said those photos were being sent straight out to the rest of the world. Then someone suggested a jumping-in-the-air group photograph and I cringed, deep and long, as we leapt with maniacal grins on our faces. When the lenses were lowered we all clamoured in to check each freshly taken photo. I wanted to see how I looked: it mattered. If it's not obsessive thoughts about sex which pull you out of the moment, it's obsessive thoughts about how the moment'll look to the rest of the world.

As the photo shoot continued, I turned to see an elderly man in lederhosen curling his lip at a teenage girl in a dirndl on the next table, curling it like a horse for an apple, crumbs and saliva collected in his white moustache. I saw her on top of him, having fok with him on the table, then me fucking her and then me fucking him, wondering what turned me on most.

I can't do this.

Making sure no-one saw me go, I began to walk, then run, through the crowds towards the exit, which from here was just a tiny square of fading light at the end of the tent. The tears ran hot on my face, and I ran and ran, until the heave of the crowd stopped me from running anymore. Now the press of bodies was too dense and I found I could hardly walk. It was hotter and louder here, and I lost sight of the exit. With a scream, unheard over the noise from the bandstand, I realised I'd entered the Pig Pen, and a kaleidoscope of sexual violence started spinning in my vision. Tightly gripped cocks, thrust together tits, arse cheeks spread for spanking. My legs went limp but I steadied myself against the torsos of the men around me, who I guess intuited in my face that I wasn't game for a grabbing. Letting out full-throated sobs, now, I tried to edge my way back out of the crush, opening my eyes only every few seconds as I waded through knob forest. A bouncer saw me from the aisle and pulled me out of the pit by the wrists, holding me while I caught my breath, but he, too, appeared to me naked, and I turned from him and ran.

Mid stride I stopped dead. *What am I doing?* I thought, crouching on the floor near the exit and gasping. *I can't run.* Running had been my default festival tactic for too long. I'd run at Reading 2002 when Peaches had come on stage in a strap-on. I'd run at Benicassim 2006 when a girl had streaked on the beach. I'd run at Exit 2007 when I'd kept seeing Wu Tang Clan's microphone as a bulbous cock. Back then I didn't care that my friends would worry about me, or ruin their own evenings looking for me. The only thing I cared about was running, as fast as my lungs would let me, away from my thoughts.

But I couldn't do that here and now, because this was a job and I was accounted for. People would get suspicious. Erik had poured his heart and soul into producing this amazing project, and I couldn't let him down. So I dried my face and walked back to the crew, and spent the next two hours giggling – full on *laughing* – through conversations about farts and morning glories and other travelling faux pas – 'ha, ha, HA, HA, I KNOW RIGHT?' – while successive waves of anxiety cut welts down my throat.

Did the others notice that something was wrong? No, or at least not enough to ask. My duplicity was a well-oiled machine, and it was the only means by which I could go on. I had to be everything I was *supposed* to be: get up when the others got up, eat when the others ate, dance when the others danced. As long as I was smiling in all the right places I could keep a lid on things.

But would I be able to keep up the ruse with even Toby?

The bus was charging on through Eastern Europe, and soon I'd be seeing him in Goa – couples' paradise. It *had* to be a dream holiday – nothing short of a Sandals advert would do. The stakes were especially high, since, in flying out to meet me, Toby would be missing the most important event of his career so far: a big awards ceremony in London in which a music video he'd recently directed had been nominated. The professional recognition meant the world to him and I was touched by his preparedness to drop it all for me. This holiday had to be perfect.

But perfection doesn't really go hand in hand with dark secrets. I tried once again to imagine how I'd word the truth if I let down my walls and told him: 'I see sexual images in my mind', 'I imagine people naked' – everything sounded fucking crazy, and right now, an entire duplicitous lifetime seemed like a rosier prospect than thwarting our holiday with those most unromantic words.

In Bulgaria we stopped the bus for the night in a car park on a remote stretch of road. There were three articulated lorries parked up but the cabins were dark and no-one was in them. The crew huddled together in little groups, secretly frottaging like loons in my mind as they walked towards the building at the centre of the car park, looking for refreshments and a bathroom. As we got closer I saw crenellated turrets, and paused. Something didn't feel right. It looked like a castle, but fake somehow – it was too regular and too new. *Is that fibreglass?* My palms began to sweat. Hanging behind the rest of the group I edged closer, watching the building for signs of life. *Why no windows?* Because whatever happened inside those walls was meant to be hidden, secret.

Debbie Does Dudley

2003. Dudley. Centre of the country and the world. I was sat with my friends at Gala Bingo in the old Hippodrome – a huge, art deco memorial to what the Midlands once were. Local campaigners with memories of greatness have stood beneath its heights to fend off the bulldozers, and won – it still stands, but look north or south or east or west from the top of Darby's Hill, at towns once rippling with men at work, and you can't help but see the flatness.

'Two fat ladies. One little duck. One and three, unlucky for some.'

I was 17, at college, and I'd split up with Greg by then. All the repellent images that'd swam into my vision and clouded his face had made moments of tenderness a little awkward. Each Valentine's Day gift ribbon had unravelled to reveal a naked kid or some other obscenity; each romantic photo, framed and offered as a love token, had animated itself into an orgy and looped in my mind like a gif, churning beneath my thank you hugs and my I love yous. During those eye-gazing moments that you're supposed to look back on as the most precious and exciting of your life, my cyclonic mind had been whirling with unspeakable stuff. I remember the pervasive David Gray soundtrack and the Ikea bed linen with the turquoise stripes; the sour-sweet smell of

Liebfraumilsch, the Natural Collection white musk candles – and the paedophilia thoughts.

Having hoped – as I'd hope countless times in the future – that if I changed my circumstances, my thoughts would change, too, I'd got myself a new boyfriend now. Our relationship was sweet and caring, but my life's duality was already cemented – already there was a gulf between the real and the performed, and it made intimacy unachievable.

Above me in the Hippodrome's grand circle and around me in the stalls, pickled octogenarians filled pints with fag ash, and waiters in dickie bows brought drinks in plastic cups from the bar, weaving among a thousand bowed heads – a sea of blue rinse. Bingo was carrying on around me, but I wasn't a part of it. I was thinking not of numbers but of tits, my friends' tits and everyone's tits.

'Dirty Gertie. Number thirty.'

No! Why am I thinking this? These girls were my friends, school friends – people I'd grown up with. I sat squirming in secret, trying to focus on the jabber of the bingo caller and trying *not* to focus on what I'd seen, as you might try, right now, not to think of a pink elephant. Or a pink elephant's tits. But each time I pressed the soft ball of the red bingo marker onto the pulpy page, I saw my friends' nipples bleed out in thread-veins into the pores, so that I couldn't look up to meet their eyes, or swallow my Cheeky Vimto.

Am I enjoying these thoughts?

No.

No.

No.

Then why can't I stop thinking them?

What do they mean?

They must mean something.

I wrung my hands under the table and shredded my thumbs. *Oh God. What is this?* My thoughts had always been about paedophilia: no tits to speak of. This had never happened before, and it was frightening in a new and different way.

Back at home that evening, after another filth-besmeared dinner of boiled potatoes and fried eggs, I sat down to watch the most innocuous TV programme I could find – Ray Mears – hoping to snatch a few minutes' respite from the thoughts, which had now been churning for several hours. But as the camera panned down across a bracken-strewn cliff face, each crevice became a startlingly detailed vagina, complete with decorative lichen. I froze, spat my mouthful of crème caramel back into the plastic pot, and looked in the mirror. 'Am I gay?' I whispered, steaming up the glass.

No answer came, so I asked again. And again, nothing came. I even asked the dog, holding her head and stretching her cheeks into a grin, 'Am I gay, dog?'

Within minutes the question had taken on a pathological urgency, and I was already scouring my memory for some kind of answer. That time when I was 11 and I felt a tingle 'down there' when I watched the bouncy boob song on *Eurotrash* – did that mean I was gay? Peeking at the breast-feeding women outside nursery, all those years ago. Did that mean I was gay?

By the next night the doubts had not stopped, so I went round to the new boyf's house and tried to use my attraction to him as a way of figuring out whether or not they were legitimate. When I kissed him guiltily at the door, the felt lettering of his *Debbie Does Dudley* T-shirt bristled under my fingers, but mercifully I didn't understand the joke. While he chatted about his day I focused on the movements of his lips and shoulders, carefully scanning my body for sensations, hoping for some Hollywood swoon to wash over me and disprove my new worries – Hollywood says that when you know, you just *know*. Follow your heart, it says. But I was concentrating so hard on how I felt in response to his every little last mannerism that I began to panic about my lack of feelings, and that made the doubts worse, and that made me *feel* worse, and then I could only think about one thing: me feeling like this is *proof* that the doubts must be real.

I drove home listening to the Rage Against The Machine cassette that Ted'd made me, digging my nails into the steering wheel. It was time to have a talk with myself, time to lay down the facts. *Think. Think. Think. Figure this all out.* Me, a gay woman? I tried to take myself there, tried to really imagine it hard. I said the word 'gay' out loud to see how it fit, I imagined myself falling in love and making love and growing old as a lesbian, but something in my mind was jarring, something wouldn't budge – the idea of being romantically involved with a woman felt elementally and insurmountably un-Me. My straightness was a fact, I was sure of it: If Destroyed Still True. But for a fact – apparently so objective and irrefutable – it was inexplicably confusing. My thoughts were contradicting who I knew I was, but weren't my thoughts also 'Me'?

I hit the steering wheel with my palm. Cat's-eyes raced

past and disappeared into the dark. *Why are sexual thoughts about women suddenly frightening?* I'd always been comfortable finding women sexy, and I was passionately pro-gay rights. In my *bones* I believed that homophobia was sinister and anti-human, and that gay love was as natural as any other kind of love.

So why was I so terrified?

Who am I? Who am I? Who am I? By the time I got home I'd shouted that question over forty minutes of foaming funk metal, driving myself further from the answer with every country mile.

From that night on, a new chapter. Now, all of a sudden, every minute of every day, I wasn't thinking about kids naked – that was gone, *completely* superseded – I was thinking about grown men and women naked, always feeling compelled to figure out which thoughts turned me on the most. The dinner lady or the headmaster? The lollypop lady or the policeman? Cherie Blair or Tony Blair?

I was meticulous in my problem solving. Many times over the next few weeks I went up to One Stop to look at *Attitude* and *Diva*, waiting for an answer to rise up from the centre folds. And over the next few months, as I started to more seriously consider the baffling possibility that I might indeed be gay, I started to 'try out' gayness in my head, bouncing to college some mornings like Pinocchio to school, telling myself that today would be the day I accepted my *true* sexuality. Hi diddle dee dee, a lesbian life for me. On other days, I would be unequivocally straight, using my relationship history as indisputable proof of that fact – citing it to myself a thousand times a day if I needed to, in response to each new doubt.

As the year progressed, nothing changed, save for my anxiety levels, which often seemed to rise when I thought they could rise no more. I chalked this frightening phenomenon up to suppression – I figured I must be suppressing something very deep-rooted, and that my anxiety would go away if I unburdened myself. So I started to tell my friends about my gay thoughts and use their reactions to gauge the plausibility of my homosexuality. I once 'came out' to Jack, and his utter disbelief temporarily assuaged my confusion. Jack had known me my whole life – our dads had been to school together. So if *he* was struggling to believe that I was gay, maybe I really wasn't. *Who am I? Who am I? Who am I?*

But still nothing changed. And still I intensified my hunt for an answer. I'd stare searchingly into my own eyes in the mirror, night after night, to try and discern what was happening 'deep down'. I'd browse profiles on lesbian dating sites, trying to imagine myself kissing each stranger's face. I'd oscillate between periods of intense immersion in sexual content, during which I hoped my brain would settle on black or white, to periods of total avoidance, during which I wouldn't even watch TV or read the paper, in an attempt to starve the sex out of my head and the anxiety from my chest.

And all the while university was looming on my horizon, a place of hedonism and narcotics where my real identity would surely reveal itself.

I'd flunked my Oxford interview because I'd been too distracted by my doubts to prepare, and when the fustian professor had interrogated me about my favourite books, I'd sat there gormless and unable to answer as his jowls flapped in front of me like a pensioner's battered plums. In truth I hadn't even wanted to go to Oxford. Duality, again: I only went to the interview as a performance because that's what I was *supposed* to do, all the while knowing that I simply wouldn't have been able to do the work – I wouldn't have been able to concentrate on the lectures and the books and writing, because my head was so full of woopie there wasn't room for anything else.

So, a year after the gay thoughts had started, I headed off to study literature at Leeds (where I thought dossing might be easier) having unceremoniously dumped Debbie Does Dudley a couple of weeks before. I'd decided by now that as my doubts were so viciously undermining my every attempt at romance, there was no point having a relationship with a boy at all. Yet, terrifyingly, there didn't seem to be an alternative, because whenever I tried to imagine a relationship with a girl, at some visceral level I balked.

By the time I arrived at uni in September 2004, I felt oddly futureless.

It was an overcast day. Me and Mom and Dad were struggling to find a parking space outside my halls of residence and I was glad to have a few extra minutes' watching from the car. On the green in front of my block, two girls – new students, I guessed – shook hands and introduced themselves to each other with breezy confidence. I'd never seen people that looked like them before. They both had golden-ish highlights and kind of backcombed hair. One's was gathered in a messy bun on top of her head and the other's was swept way over to one side like a mane. They were both white and super-tanned and kind of freckly, and they both had on these beige-brown slipper boot things which I'd never seen before either. One had on a netball skirt, but I think it was just for fashion.

I looked down at my green corduroy bootcuts and wondered whether I'd made a good choice.

The Fiesta door squeaked loudly when Dad opened the boot, and some stuff fell out – an old, yellowing duvet and pillow, and some rolled up posters – and the two girls started walking over to help. I really didn't want them to, because no-one in my family is that good at casual chitchat, but they carried on walking over, saying these big cheerful 'hellos', like the trendy moms used to do at the school gates.

When they bent down to help us pick up the stuff I caught a glimpse of the netball one's thighs, almost right up to her bum, and I winced all through my 'thank yous', and all through the bit where she asked me where I was from, and all through my goodbyes with my parents. And all through that night and the next day, and all through Freshers' Week. All the time thinking, thinking, thinking, about those long, tanned, freckly thighs.

Why am I imagining them?

What do they mean?

Who am I?

And as the semester wore on and the doubts intensified further, an enormous question started forming in my mind: if I tried it with a girl, just once, maybe I'd find an answer?

Cork-Sole Wedges

As we walked across the Bulgarian tarmac, approaching the mock-goth doorway of the windowless building, we noticed red neon fringing on one of the turrets. I locked my legs and wouldn't walk any further, but the rest of the crew trotted on, wide-eyed, realising.

'Oh my God.'

'This kinda looks like a brothel.'

'AMAYzing.'

I felt faint at the thought of what might be inside, but followed them in. No choice really. I couldn't risk staying in the bus and arousing suspicion.

We bumbled through the doors and stopped dead. Pin-drop silence in a vast banquet hall. A handful of truckers eyeballed us, open-mouthed, fags hanging from their lips. A playing card fluttered silently to the floor but no-one looked at it. We'd interrupted a game of poker.

We stood in the doorway in silence, shuffling our feet. We didn't see the small man behind the bar until he darted out of a back door. Rustling sounds and whispers. Then a plump woman rushed out smiling and squealing, flapping her hands at the men around the table in a 'take no notice of them' sort of way. She made 'hello' sounds and flashed us giant, wrinkled smiles as she gleefully showed us to one of the cartwheel tables.

Her grey-streaked hair was pulled back into a scrunchy and she wore silver eyeshadow with candy pink lipstick. Her Lycra sports jacket was zipped right to the top, bulging over a diamante belt and distressed bootcut jeans. She wore pink socks under her cork-sole wedges, which clopped on the lino as she walked back through the side door to get us beers. *Is that the madam?* I thought. Porn had lead me to believe that madams wore more satin corsetry and much more silicone. I scanned my body for sensations. Anxiety? Arousal? Nothing *too* severe. I was doing okay so far.

We looked at each other and around the room, wide-eyed. The vast strip-lit hall was uncannily sparse, with a pastiche of furniture: vigorously distressed wooden chairs around large tables, and antler chandeliers bearing plastic red candles.

Four new women came out of the side door, smiling, with a beer in each hand, and as they placed the bottles on the table, releasing their fingers from the beer's wet sides, I saw the schlongs of all the truckers I imagined they'd touched, and I faked a sneeze to justify the sudden tears in my eyes. The others joked with them, cheersing them and trying to speak Bulgarian. So I did too, playing my part.

More men appeared from the side door and started setting up instruments, and before long they had a full-blown Bulgarian disco going, with Middle Eastern percussive beats, a keyboardist and a clarinet player. Two moustached locals took to the dance floor, clapping their hands and shouting, 'Hey! Hey! Hey!' A clarinettist, who was somehow playing and shaking his tits at the same time, got to his knees to serenade the band of ladies dancing around him, who feigned coyness when he winked at them. Soon everyone was dancing, even me, though I made pains to avoid the most beautiful of the ladies. The vibrato vocal reached crescendo.

This is exactly the kind of off-kilter edge that everyone's digital profile needs: a party in a brothel complete with plastic-clad prostitutes, rotund punters and borderline-trendy Euro-beats. We knew its power. Someone took a video and posted it on Facebook and the next day words like 'epic' and 'crazy' abounded, and the comments were full of the desired envy.

The omitted truth was that we barely stayed an hour, and were tucked up and asleep like giant babies by 10pm.

Setting my teeth against the graphic, pimp-filled images which lumbered at me as the bus chugged towards Asia, I mulled over this tendency of ours to falsify, and used it as solace. Having wanted, since the doubts first started, to be wholly present in each moment and wholly engrossed in a collective experience, I now wondered whether collective experience was just an illusion. If how something looks online is more important than how it feels in real life, maybe no-one else was completely 'here' either. Maybe everyone was so invested in the portrayal of their experience that they were as far removed from it as I was. Maybe the gulf between my outward life and my inner life was just like the schism I saw all around me: the gulf between who we are and who we want people to think we are.

Titgate

Leeds. The mid-noughties. Nu Rave was about to explode in the North, Facebook hadn't happened yet, and the now-ubiquitous skinny jean was slowly filtering down into the mainstream. Definite article bands like The Strokes and The White Stripes and The Hives, which'd sound-tracked so many college house parties, were still a solid centre-left choice for any teenager with vague alternative aspirations. But something new was rippling through a million MySpace profiles. The sound was electro, and bass-laced synthetic dance pop would soon start streaming in from producers in Paris, dizzying the twenteens of Britain with its accessible, anthemic funk. Everywhere, all over the country, indie kids would start to dance.

The mid-noughties, as anyone who was young and desperate to be cool at the time will remember, were also notable for the rise of American Apparel – the high street fashion retailer with a penchant for Lycra and high waists, and for employing shrivelled male scenesters to photograph barely-post-pubescent girls in panties for ad campaigns – ad campaigns that students saw in skate magazines and thought the epitome of louche-cool.

Leeds was a place to be young, a playground. If I was going to find my illusive Self anywhere it would be here – sexual exploration was part of the aesthetic, after all, and hedonism was there for the aping. So a couple of weeks after my parents dropped me off, when I'd finally stopped obsessing about netball girl's thighs and sobbing to 'Wild World' in my room, I started testing the sexual waters, for want of a better expression.

By now firmly believing that I was experiencing a sexual identity crisis – there was simply *no other* explanation for the recurrence of my doubts – I amped up my quest to figure out how a gay or bisexual identity might go down. I spent the first semester throwing out phrases like 'sometimes I'm in the mood for chocolate, sometimes I'm in the mood for vanilla' and other *howlingly* cringe-worthy euphemisms for 'bi-curiosity', and once again used my friends' reactions as a way of judging if I sounded authentic.

One morning I went to campus to check out the fabled 'free shop', where you could literally just *take* stuff, which was just about the coolest and most bohemian thing I'd ever heard. On the way back, laden with piles of swag, including an American baseball helmet and an inflatable palm tree, I bumped into a girl from my halls.

'Hey Rachel, how you doing,' I said. 'Hey' was something new I was trying out.

'Yeah, good, thanks, you alright?'

'Yeah, great, ta, you?'

'Yeah good, thanks.'

'Cool.'

'How are you? What you been up to?'

And so the casual chitchat went on.

Rachel was funny. From Newcastle and dry as a fucking bone. Often she regaled me with updates of her parents' midlife crises and farcical snippets from local Tyneside news. Today she was talking totally deadpan about how much money she'd spent in the hair salon achieving the *perfect* shade of mouse, and extolling the many practical uses of inflatable palm trees.

The morning sun was soft on her face, and as she talked an image flashed into my mind of me kissing her. Instant anxiety in my throat.

Maybe I fancy her.

I don't know. I think I fancy boys.

But I imagined kissing her – what does that mean?

I don't think it means anything.

But it might mean I'm attracted to her physically.

Maybe I want to have sex with her.

No, I think I like boys.

But I'm THINKING about having sex with her so I MUST fancy her.

'Anyway, gotta run,' she said, and walked off, smiling.

'Maybe I like boys *and* girls,' I repeated to myself fifty times as I walked back to my halls, trying to put a full stop to my spiralling thoughts.

Due to our mutual friends, Rachel and I hung out often. Groups of us would go down to the student union for school disco parties and Karl Kennedy from *Neighbours* concerts. Then we'd pile back to someone's kitchen – papered with Ministry of Silly Walks and Le Chat Noir posters, and watch late night *Hollyoaks* episodes or lie around in someone's bedroom and watch obligatory cult movies that everyone pretended to be more familiar with than they actually were. My folks' reliable filmic diet of *Room With A View, Last Of*

The Mohicans and anything with Kenneth Branagh, meant that I had more pretending to do than most. I distinctly remember saying 'oh, I love this bit' when Withnail got arrested, having never of course seen the film. But the resounding and probably equally dishonest 'me tooooooooos' made the falsification totally worth it.

Each time I saw Rachel, or heard her name mentioned, or saw someone on the street that looked like her, I was reminded about that first day when I'd thought about kissing her. I'd have to stop whatever I was doing and hold an image of her in my mind while scanning my body for sensations and clues (this checking tactic had now become habitual). And in doing so, I was so often rewarded with nervous twitches – twitches which felt a bit like, but also nothing like, arousal. *Perhaps these feelings, and the fact that I think about her so much, are PROOF that I like her romantically.* It felt like the more I ruminated, the more I cemented that possibility in my mind; the more I stared at her, waiting for a sense of certainty to wash over me, the more racked with doubt I became.

I didn't feel like I fancied her in the way that I was used to fancying boys – the flutters and the flirting and the skipping in the street. I'd never swooned for her or felt an involuntary shy smile sweep across my face for her. But I chalked that absence up to the fact that I hadn't actually *tried* fancying her yet – maybe if I tried, y'know . . . I'd realise that I'd actually been into girls all along. And if I knew *that*, then I'd finally know who I was.

One evening a big group of us had all been out drinking at a pound-a-pint night, where I'd spent eight pounds. I was already deep into my Lycra phase, and that night I'd chosen black, high-waisted lamé leggings with cowl-necked stiletto boots and a crop top, the kind of outfit Dad quietly sighed over when I fussed in front of the lounge mirror. Rightly so, I now concede.

Having tried to avoid her all night, I ended up chatting to Rachel through bleary eyes for a couple of pints, swallowing down the sequential lumps which rose in my throat when she brushed my arm or squeezed my leg for emphasis. *Maybe I should just go for it*, I'd thought, at least fifty times a pint. At this point memory's already sketchy, but I do remember teetering to the toilet and, in a quite staggering feat of self-absorption and teenage angst, scrawling Blake's *The Sick Rose* with my marker onto the toilet wall.

O Rose thou art sick.
The invisible worm,
That flies in the night
In the howling storm:

Has found out thy bed
Of crimson joy:
And his dark secret love
Does thy life destroy.

And I was sick 'n' all. Eight pints sick. Could Blake ever have predicted that his sublime verse would be co-opted by a bewildered wannabe-scenester, holding back the wisps of her noughties mullet while she vomited into a seatless and pube-speckled loo?

Back in Rachel's room later that night, a few of us stayed up chatting on her bed – just *hangin'*, you know, being cool – and gradually the group dwindled until just three of us were left: Rachel, our other hallmate Becky, and me. *America's Next Top Model* – which brought with it its own anxieties – was on quietly in the background while we chatted.

Soon Becky announced that she was too tired to go back to her own bed and took off her T-shirt to get comfy. As she did so, she did a comedy tit-shake, and Rachel poked Becky's bra as a child might. Then Rachel took off her own sweater and shook her tits around, too, laughing, pissed out of her mind, humming a kind of swing-y, can-can song. Then Becky and Rachel kind of kissed, although not really because they were spluttering and laughing too much. And because I was young and definitely not frigid, and this is what young and unfrigid people do, I joined in. Then we were all sitting in our bras and laughing (me utterly forcedly) and poking each other's wabs and belly rolls, and blowing raspberries and snogging. At one point someone was singing Junior Murvin's 'Police and Thieves' and the whole thing, tonally, was less porno pyjama party and more Smell Bums: the Teenage Edition. It's possible that someone even trumped at one point. Oh baby, baby, it's a wild world.

Curiously, I didn't feel particularly anxious. Rather: totally numb – just pissed and disillusioned in a Holden Caulfield kind of way. When I touched their bodies I felt as much relish as a butcher slapping hams, *but*, I thought through the booze, *BUT THIS IS IT. This is what I have to do. This is necessary.* If I was ever going figure out who I was, I needed to push this further, further, further. The next few minutes could give me a *definitive* answer about who I was – a definitive resolution to my identity. This could be my chance finally discover the truth and stop the ambiguous thoughts and the terrible anxiety for ever and ever, and then tomorrow will be the start of my new life—

'Should we ... y'know ...' I asked Rachel, slurring, raising crooked eyebrows.

Sudden silence in the room.

'Err ... no,' was the resounding, unequivocal reply. And that was that.

When I woke up the morning after – the first morning of my new life of certainty – I stood at the mirror, squinting past the lipstick smears I'd made during many a Robert Palmer 'Addicted to Love' moment, and took a contrived, deep breath. 'That's it,' I said aloud, exhaling, 'I tried to have lesbian sex and I wasn't into it, so now we know: I'm straight.'

Am I sure about that?

Yes.

Am I 100% certain?

Maybe not.

I sat down on the bathroom floor, and immediately began playing last night's scene over and over in my mind, trying to determine how I'd *really* felt.

Maybe the fact I even CONSIDERED having lesbian sex means I'm gay.

I don't think it means anything.

But I'm thinking about it NOW, so it must mean something.

Maybe even having these thoughts IS proof that I'm gay.

But I wasn't aroused, so I can't be.

*But just because I didn't enjoy it ONE TIME doesn't
mean anything.*

Maybe if I tried it again I'd have an answer.

*Maybe the fact I even CONSIDERED having lesbian sex
means I'm gay.*

And so on. And so on. And so on.

I couldn't believe it. Since the gay doubts had started, over
18 months ago, I'd always presumed that they'd go away if
I just *proved* the answer to myself with concrete results. But
now I'd taken a pretty definitive test and I was as desperately confused as ever.

Fuckfuckfuck. I needed more evidence.

Sexcetera

The upstairs room was darkly lit by amber lights overhead. I was sat on a padded seat in a Birmingham strip club, drunk like Dumbo, smashed out of my face on cheap white wine. A naked woman who called herself Susie was dancing in front of me.

It was over a year since Titgate and a couple of years since Debbie Does Dudley, and though I was objectively no closer to an answer about who I was, I was still finding myself drawn to men, and I'd relented on my resolve not to get into a relationship.

I had a new sort-of boyfriend now. We had English lectures together and had bonded over the books we loved. In the early hours we'd speak in juvenile but heartfelt literary tropes about our respective feelings of outsidership, reading Nietzsche and Larkin and Nabokov. Often, we'd cheerily chew the fat about what Steinbeck called the Welshrats: a feeling of sadness about the state of the world, crawling like rats in your belly.

I loved him, but I was insecure and immature, and I looked to him for affirmation and commitment that he couldn't give me, making myself sick with jealousy over the other women he was seeing.

When you're young and you love someone and you're

distressed, your problems feel like their fault. Because Hollywood told us to hold out for heroes. Because Hollywood told us that the emotional salvation of girls lay in men. Because Hollywood told us that love conquers all. And as I tried to tick romance's boxes – wearing his T-shirts, walking on the moors, smoking cigarettes under the stars – love was failing. Because I was unhappy and he couldn't mend me.

Years later I'd find a little phrase in Milan Kundera's *The Unbearable Lightness of Being* – 'Her weakness was aggressive' – and think of this time and this quasi-relationship. I would realise that you can overpower someone with your vulnerability, and I'd vow never to do it again.

Recently, unknown to him, and to everyone else who knew me, I'd spent every minute alone engaged in an endless spiralling search, a search I realised made absolutely no rational sense, but which I was unable to stop: comparing male and female nude photography anthologies; reading *The Story of O* and *The Story of the Eye* and *The Sexual Confessions of Catherine M.*; watching *9 Songs* and *Sexcetera*, and writing 'coming out' mantras every day. Now, every time I had a sexual thought, I was responding with the phrase, 'I'm definitely gay, I'm definitely gay, I'm definitely gay,' in an attempt to force my brain into settling on a conclusion.

But nothing was working long term and any sense of an 'answer' was fleeting. The more I searched, the more I felt my identity crumble. My emotions became fey and hysterical. When I laughed I laughed maniacally and for a long time. I felt a way that only a person who's felt insane can understand – not of myself, bodiless, watching myself.

The word 'obsession' comes from the Latin *obsidere*

which means 'to besiege', and if this siege continued indefinitely I was fairly sure I would soon die. Not that I'd yet thought intently about suicide. I mean, I literally couldn't visualise being alive for much longer if I couldn't figure out who I was. Like, if you think about all the time in history before you were born – the fall of Carthage or the storming of the Bastille or the first time your parents met – what did all those centuries feel like? They felt like nothing, because you just didn't exist. And that's how I felt about my future, as a sort of death in its truest sense: an extinction of Self.

So I decided to enter what I believed to be the lion's den of women's sexuality – the strip club – and find the answer which would save my life. I needed to get to its sweaty heart: the dressing room, where, if porn had educated me honestly, the flower of female eroticism bloomed.

Luckily I had an in: a friend of mine was a stripper at a club in Birmingham town centre, a wreckhead, chat-at-parties kind of friend rather than a heart-to-heart, McVitie's kind of friend, but she was fun and I adored her. She was smart, carefree and comfortable with her sexuality. She loved stripping and the money it made her, and she considered it a no-brainer career move for any young woman who wanted to get ahead. Several times she'd entreated me to at least 'come and have a look' at her workplace and see what I thought. I might see the upsides, she'd said.

So one day I agreed, faking interest in job prospects for the sake of gaining access to this potentially mind-altering venue. *This is my chance*, I thought. *There I'll find the answer.*

*

The day came round much sooner than I would've liked, and I'd drunk a bottle of Echo Falls before I stepped, almost stumbled, into the club. My friend guided me through the dimly lit main room like an estate agent, pointing out the poles and the booths and a stage fringed with blue lights.

'And here's the dressing room,' she said, holding open the door.

I took a deep, Hollywood breath, a moment-of-truth breath, a this-is-it breath, in the hope of bringing about a definitive change in consciousness. *Here I am*, I thought. *The next few minutes will dictate my future.*

I stepped inside. The room was starkly lit with strip lights, and was lined with benches and lockers – more five-a-side than French boudoir. There were women in various states of undress and I scanned the sensations in my body, searching for clues as to how they made me feel. They chatted while they changed their outfits. Receptionists and personal trainers and shop managers in their teens and twenties and thirties, chatting about their day jobs and their families. They snapped their thongs against their buttocks, dimpled in the harsh lighting, plumping their breasts into ill-fitting bras and slipping on plastic heels and plastic dresses. There were black women and white women and Asian women, skinny women and chubby women, a couple of blondes, a brunette and a redhead. Something for every punter.

Looking at them intently I forcibly exhaled, listening to my body and my mind. Nothing.

Vague panic. How could *this* place not give me an answer?

I'm definitely gay, I'm definitely gay, I'm definitely gay, I shouted in my mind as I stared at the women, trying to bring about an irrefutable conclusion.

Still no answer.

I caught a glimpse of myself in a mirror and felt the first swell of boozy sadness. I was wearing the black dress my sister Maggie had bought me from a sample sale in her office. A *sample sale*, in her *office*. Down in London's media world. I'd always coveted her sample sales and her Whistles jerseys and her Wagamama meals, which blew me away with their glamour when I went to visit her. I'd always coveted the beauty and warmth and grace she'd inherited from our mother. She was who I'd always wanted to be. But I wasn't Maggie. I wasn't even myself. And I couldn't see any further into my future than this definitive night.

'You should get a dance,' my friend said, taking me by the hand. 'I think Susie's already on the floor, she's amazing.'

My throat burned.

'I dunno—'

'—it's cool, you should see how it's done so you can make your mind.'

I WISH I could make up my mind.

And then there she was: the amazing Susie, butt naked and writhing at my lap, her flesh prompting in me nothing but numbness – a deflation so physical, so palpable that it quite overrode my cacophonous thoughts, my whole body so chemically underwhelmed by my heart's failure to flutter, by the earth's failure to shake.

This is not how it's supposed to be.

I'm supposed to KNOW by now.

I'm definitely gay.

I'm definitely gay.
I'm definitely gay.
Nothing.

When Susie finished she seemed pleased with herself and raised her eyebrows expectantly, as though waiting for a rating. How do you tell someone with puppy dog eyes that their pum didn't cut it?

'Errrmmm . . . yep,' I said with one drunk-heavy nod. She laughed, puzzled, and led me back downstairs. I wanted to leave but my friend encouraged me to stay for a drink.

Sat in my dress on a plastic stool, I drank two large glasses of white Blossom Hill, so that by the time the punters came in I barely remembered where I was or why I was here. My memories are unconnected images – a grisly punter trying to talk to me, the cubicle floor flecked with tears, the blurs of trying to walk – and then a rush of clarity and action, bumbling down the spiral staircase saying' 'I've made a mistake, I've made a mistake, I've made a mistake' to my bewildered friend.

I told a handful of people a very specific version of this story afterwards, in accordance with the version of myself that I was putting out into the world. The surface Me was a sexually liberated modern woman, adventurous and nonchalant, like the bohemiennes in *The Story of O* and *The Story of The Eye* who lapped milk from saucers and wore pearls when getting paddled by powerful men. I spoke about that night like it'd just been a game and a 'bit of fun', like I'd been comfortable 'checking out the scene.' But my casual shrugs belied the truth.

And I can never forget the feeling of the Welshrats

gnawing at my guts as the realisation washed over me: having taken a man's world definition of female eroticism for granted and gone in search of my life's defining, unequivocal sexual moment, I once again felt sexless and sad, and more lost than ever.

Shit Disco

10.55am – English exam. The following spring. 'How does John Donne use metaphysics to advance his themes in the *Holy Sonnets*?' The page was blank. I was watching the clock with heavy eyelids. Five minutes to go.

It was the last of several exams testing our understanding of Renaissance literature and I'd walked out of every one so far. You can't leave an exam until one hour after its official start.

Two minutes to go.

11am – I picked up my heavy body and walked slowly out, my boots scuffing on the wooden floors. It was a public declaration of failure, watched by 200 people whose bodies I'd undressed, inch by inch, during wasted John Donne lectures, week after week after week.

I stepped into the blustery, overcast morning onto the quiet campus. It was one of those loud-silent days where the high winds drown out every other sound. Students skulked, here and there – fellow dropouts I imagined – guilty like jackals. Leaves whooshed in the gardens. I sat on a bench outside the School Of English, eating Campinos and watching the swell of a distant tree.

I had two slow hours to kill before my doctor's appointment.

The wonderful creaminess of the Campinos was welcome on two counts. One: I was hungry, having thrown up my food every night for six months. Two: I was so tripped out on escitalopram – an SSRI anti-depressant – that my senses were numbed, and those exquisite little sweeties, with their juicy layers of red and white, reminded me that I was indeed a human, with feet on this earth and breath in my lungs. I rolled the smooth sweet against my teeth, counting each click click as it passed the ridges. The tree fretted in the wind somewhere far away.

The doctor's appointment was a follow-up to one I'd had a few months earlier. I'd gone because in the wake of my little strip club chuff-hunt, the feeling of futurelessness had grown into a sense of ever-rising doom. I was single again, and lonely. *Maybe I'm depressed because I can't accept who I am*, I'd thought, a thousand times a day. I'd read that the coming out process often leads to mental distress, and that doctors could prescribe something to make it easier.

1pm – 'How are you feeling, Rose?'

'I've quit uni.'

'I'm sorry to hear that.' His voice sounded muffled, like my skull was twice as thick as normal. 'How have you come to that decision?'

'I—'

'Have you been keeping up with the escitalopram?'

'Yes, I—'

'Good. Have you seen any improvement in the anxiety?'

'I don't know.' I really didn't know. It was hard to think

through the fog. 'Nothing's really changed, it's just all a bit cloudier and mufflier.'

'Are you still purging?'

'Sorry?'

'Are you still vomiting after meals? You said last time you'd been eating chocolate bars every night and throwing them up. Is that still happening?'

'No, it's—'

'Well, that's progress, then.'

'—ice cream.'

'Excuse me?'

'I throw up chocolate *ice cream*. It's softer.'

'I see. And you're still doing it every day? Any other types of purging, like laxatives?'

'Yes, a whole tub after dinner every day. No laxatives. It's got worse since I went on the tablets.'

'Sometimes it does take a while for them to settle into your system.'

'I don't—'

'If I asked you to compare the way you feel now to the way you felt six months ago, could you put a percentage on the difference?'

'Sorry?'

'You know, 40% better, 50% better?' he encouraged.

'Erm . . .' I thought hard, confused. 'I don't think it's as simple as that.'

'Excuse me?'

'Well, I don't feel better at all, I just feel like a zombie. The doubting thoughts are still just as bad. And I don't know if I can rate my feelings with a single figure.'

I raised my head to look at him, and there was the face –

the face I've seen on so many doctors since. The righteous face. The how-dare-you face. The don't-you-know-who-I-am face.

I imagined him sitting naked in just his socks.

'And I'm cutting myself,' I said, rolling up my sleeve and holding out my arm. On its underside were five inches of cuts. Five deep ones about an inch apart and shallower ones between them. 'Because I don't feel anything and when I cut, it hurts, and it makes me feel like a human again. I haven't shed a tear for six months.'

'Yes, that's not an uncommon side effect.'

My eyelids felt heavy again. The image of him naked flashed up once more. Now he was doing the willy dance.

I'm not turned on.

That doesn't mean anything.

But maybe if I was straight I WOULD be.

I don't have to be attracted to EVERY member of the opposite sex.

The image flashed again. Now he was slapping his penis on the keyboard.

I'm still not turned on.

That doesn't mean anything.

He was writing something out on his prescription pad. More of the same drugs. *Is that it? No therapy? Just tranqs?* How could I make him understand? This person who held the keys to the gate? For the first time I felt that feeling that anyone's who's experienced depression will have felt: that longing for the bleeding wound or the fractured bone. The straight-up-and-down brokenness of injury. Here it is. Look at it. Tell me what you see. Fix it.

'Keep up with your dosage and your herbal tea and breathing,' he said as I shuffled out the door, 'and I'll see you again in six months.'

I left the surgery and went home to think. 'Take time to think,' they say, 'think things through,' 'get some headspace.' I was going to re-take my uni year in September, but from now until then I would be freed to devote myself entirely to *thinking* myself out of my thoughts. I'd be able to focus on my quest for truth, uninterrupted.

10pm – A house party. Even through my doped up haze I couldn't resist an opportunity to expose myself to bodies – there was still soul-searching to be done.

By now dance music had definitely happened in Leeds, and synths were now very much *de rigueur*. Tonight a rumour had swept through uni that Shit Disco and The Rapture were playing at a house party near the campus, and we'd all descended on the red brick terrace for a night we hoped might look something like an episode of *Skins* – another notable product of 2007.

By then I'd made friends I would keep for life: 'the girls'. We'd gravitated to each other after realising we were always at the same club nights, and within weeks we were cooking meals together every Thursday and partying together every weekend. Soon they felt like family, and as such, they needed to be steadfastly protected from my messy interior life.

We arrived at the party together and dispersed into ones and twos, on missions for the toilet and mixers and the dancefloor. I couldn't be sure whether or not I'd seen any of the famous band members in the crowd, because pretty much everyone had scruffy hair and tight trousers and a trendy pigeon-toed walk. Besides, starspotting wasn't really an option. I was too sluggish, and now, too drunk, to really care.

I slumped on a chair in the back room and noticed two girls getting off with each other in the corner. By sheer force, anxiety was still able to rise above the effects of the escitalopram. They weren't kissing hornily, they were kissing tenderly and beautifully, and I envied their happiness. The Rapture's 'House Of Jealous Lovers' began playing in the next room and they got up to dance. Why, why, why, when I'd opened myself up so completely to gayness, couldn't I just accept who I was? *If I'm gay then it's fine. It's fucking fine. I'm definitely gay, I'm definitely gay, I'm definitely gay,* I thought, taking another swig of Jägermeister. *What the hell's the problem?*—

'Oi. You're the girl who walks out of English exams, aren't you?' a boy slurred.

'Yes,' I said, walking out. *That's exactly who I am.*

Sheltering on the doorstep I unwrapped a Campino and put it in my mouth and held it against the roof of my mouth. It was juicy and delicious.

In the streets I watched the old Leeds cobbles crawl underneath me as I walked, flinching from rapidfire mental images of those gay girls having fok on the dancefloor. I was exhausted. First months of trying to believe that I was straight. Then months of trying to believe that I was gay. I'd tried everything I could think of to give myself the freedom to be whatever the fuck I was, deep down. And still the doubts were as fearsome as ever. I'd now lived more than

2000 days without so much as 20 seconds free from graphic sexual mental images. From my foggy mind I could pull one coherent thought: *something is very, very wrong.*

Brown Sauce

Many years later a doctor would warn me not to discount anti-depressants based on one bad experience, because they can make some people feel better. She'd tell me that I'd clearly been given too high a dose of escitalopram, and that I might have really felt the benefits of the medication had that not been the case. She'd add that anti-depressants were most effective when teamed with cognitive behavioural therapy, and was baffled that it hadn't been offered to me in conjunction with the drugs.

But back when I was 21 and tranqued off my tits, I didn't have that kind of insight, and for me, coming off the drugs – which had done nothing to deter the ever-encroaching poontang – was a clear-cut decision.

You're supposed to wean yourself off SSRIs very slowly, to give your brain chemistry a chance to adjust. Foolishly, I didn't do this – I just stopped them dead and felt weird for days. I had trippy dreams and flinches and felt hypersensitive to sound. One night the neighbours played drum and bass until 8am and I emptied a whole bottle of brown Sauce through their letterbox, taking the bottle with me when I left to ensure they'd assume the worst about the sticky-brown squits hardening on their hallway carpet.

This is not me.

I knew that coming out could be shitty. Many times I had compulsively read coming out stories on inspirational websites, to check whether or not they sounded familiar. There I'd read tales of depression and confusion and anxiety, not unlike my own. Like me, many of these people had experienced years of self-doubt and loneliness, and I'd easily identified with their feelings. But now, thinking about those girls at that house party a week before and how utterly in love they'd seemed, our commonalities were less apparent.

Again I sat down at my desk to read the coming out tales of strangers, and this time I noticed a common theme: joy, albeit sometimes secret or beleaguered or fleeting. The people in the stories seemed to rejoice in their identities. Their delight at the idea of being freely gay and accepted for it was irrepressible – it came bubbling from the page beautifully and movingly. It was same hug-the-world joy that I'd seen in the faces of those girls.

'This is not me,' I said, lighting a fag. And even though I had no idea what was happening inside, I now knew that my brain's 24/7 screaming was something different. For the first time I suspected that I was mental – that there was an illness in my head. I could feel the mentalness in there, like my brain had corroded, unseen in the dark, eaten out by dry rot. It might look normal if you took it out – the intestine-y pink stuff might look healthy and squidgy – but if you touched the cerebrum, or shouted too loud, or shined a light too bright, it would petrify and fritter into dust.

I moved my cursor and clicked the little Xs on all my open windows, as if to clear my mind. *Mentally ill? But how? What are these thoughts?* Some kind of interference?

Some kind of stuck record in my head? What could that be? Then I Googled the words 'intrusive thoughts' and changed my life forever.

Part Two

Dirty Blu Tack

The screen flickered as I jerked my chair closer to the computer, breathless. 'Intrusive thoughts': something about these two words felt critical. I hovered over the Wikipedia link and gulped.

Click-click.

It was already dark. Outside the window a pair of Chuck Taylors flapped by their laces from the telephone wires. Someone had thrown them up there because, well – they probably didn't know why themselves, but that's just what students do. In a lamp's circle of light I huddled over my desk. Wind sucked at the window.

My housemates were downstairs watching *Hollyoaks* – a ritual I was usually a part of. The show's glut of sillybilly muscle men and braless Sharons provided ample fodder for my obsession. I'd try to figure out if I was more attracted to Mandy or Tony. I'd try to figure out which of the McQueen sisters I found prettiest. *The fact I'm even asking the question means I'm gay, surely?* I'd try to figure out if I fancied Jack Osborne, the 50-something landlord of The Dog, who once appeared shower-fresh in nothing but a towel trussed tight against his doughy belly. Surely if there was a shred of straightness in me, I, woman, would be attracted to *him*, a man, grey chest hair 'n all? These nonsensical internal ruminations would go on long after the credits had rolled, long after the pesto pasta had been devoured, and they usually wouldn't stop until they were superseded later in the evening by something more graphic, post-watershed – a doc about tit-jobs would do it. Tonight the sound of ad breaks blaring through the floor unsettled me, because my inner dramas usually happened in the dead of night when I could weep freely, safe in the knowledge that no-one would knock the door offering tea and Hobnobs.

I shut out the noise and read: 'Intrusive thoughts are unwelcome involuntary thoughts, images, or doubts that are upsetting or distressing, and can be difficult to manage or eliminate.' I gasped. *'Involuntary?'* I'd always presumed that my thoughts spoke from some deep, unconscious part of me, like they were some repressed Freudian yearning trying to breach the surface. I'd always thought that I *was* my thoughts.

Holding my breath, I darted down the page, and when I saw the subheading 'Inappropriate sexual thoughts,' I burst into silent tears. I wiped my T-shirt across my face in one movement, and read on, trembling: 'One of the more common sexual intrusive thoughts occurs when an obsessive person doubts his or her sexual identity. As with most sexual obsessions, sufferers may feel shame and live in isolation, finding it hard to discuss their fears, doubts, and concerns about their sexual identity.'

Oh my God. Still me. All me. I was sobbing now, holding my hands against my mouth, snatching breaths between the cracks of my fingers, unable to look away from the screen. There they were: my secrets, typed in sans-serif by a stranger. 'Common.' They were common? *So that means I'm not alone? I AM NOT ALONE!* I stood up and shouted three triumphant 'fucks' at myself in the mirror, then sat back down to keep reading, rapacious.

But I was distracted, again and again, by one unfamiliar phrase popping from the page: 'pure O'. There it was again. And again. And again. Peppering the prose. *What the hell is pure O?*

Click-click.

'Pure O is an anxiety disorder characterised by distressing intrusive thoughts, often of a sexual or violent nature. It is a lesser-known manifestation of OCD.'

'What? *How?*' I muttered to myself. I knew what OCD was – TV had told me everything I needed to know about it. It was people frightened of germs and dirt and light switches; the cleanfreaks and the anals. What did *that* have to do with intrusive thoughts about *sex?* I stabbed across the internet, erratic and disbelieving. Beside the mouse mat lay an ageing assortment of dirty Blu Tack, loose baccy, old keys, pennies and bills. *Fucking obsessive compulsive disorder. As if.*

I clicked on 'OCD' and read.

There it was: 'Sexuality,' right up there at the top of the page – not an afterthought or a footnote, but right up there listed as a common OCD theme alongside cleanliness and scrupulosity.

'Excessive doubts about sexual orientation are experienced by both gay and straight people with OCD, who, unlike non-sufferers, cannot dismiss intrusive sexual thoughts as random. The frequency and graphic nature of their obsessions typically causes them to assume that they're experiencing a sexual identity crisis.'

'Oh my God,' I said. I was shaking.

'This misinterpretation is confounded by the fact that the

soul-searching, mental anguish and experimentation involved in the sufferer's compulsive search for an answer so closely resemble a coming out process—'

—The *Hollyoaks* theme tune. *No!* Knocks at the door were imminent – queries as to whether I wanted to 'go in' on the bolognese or the macaroni cheese or the chili con carne. I was adept at putting on a false self in public, but it's harder to pull off when your cuticles are bleeding and your heart rate's gone gabber and your face looks like a blobfish.

I crouched down with my laptop in front of my bedroom door and tried to slow my breathing as I read on.

'For a sufferer of this manifestation of OCD, the idea of having to give up their cherished sexual identity and adopt another jars intensely with their personal desires, but the more they try to cling to their inflexible definition of self, the worse their intrusive thoughts become, and the less sure of themselves they feel. Unable to step into a sexual identity which feels unnatural to them, yet unable to enjoy their own, and finding their relationships and sex lives blighted by distressing thoughts, they become increasingly disillusioned, consumed by the terror that they may never know who they are.'

'Oh shit oh shit oh shit,' I whispered, crying laughing, happysad. It all sounded so breathtakingly accurate yet so preposterous. *Who am I? WHAT IS THIS?* If this 'pure O' OCD thing was real why hadn't I heard of it? Why had none of my friends? Why didn't people talk about it on the telly? It sounded like utter bullshit – an elaborate cover-up for being in the closet. It can't be true yet nothing in my life has ever been truer—

I stopped and gasped at the screen:

'Another common obsessive-compulsive theme is the persistent worry that one is a paedophile and might harm a child.'

Paedophilia thoughts a symptom of OCD? *Fuck.* I had never connected those adolescent anxieties about abusing kids – five years ago now – to my current worries about gayness. *Impossible.* The former had been an aberration – physically and morally abhorrent and shameful in every way – and the suggestion of parity between the two themes was a grotesque affront to my principles, it repulsed me. But here it was in black and white: 'OCD isn't about principles, it's about uncertainty.'

What am I READING? I shook my head as I tried to make sense of the words. They seemed to be saying that in both obsessive themes it was uncertainty itself that was terrifying – the possibility of never knowing your 'true identity', absolutely and categorically; that both themes were frightening because, in different ways, they both cast doubt on the most fundamental aspect of the human: the self.

Fuck me, this thing is REAL.

I took one deep breath and lay back on the carpet, my arms and legs outstretched, exhausted. The Artex swirled on the ceiling a mile above me. Now I was quiet and still and I didn't even blink – nothing moved except my heart.

Bhangra Electro

I woke up at 5am, due to meet Toby at Goa International Airport in an hour. The other crew members had dispersed to different parts of the province, and I was here alone. In the shower I tried to focus on the water pressure on my back and breathe deeply.

You don't get much more hyped than airport reunions. In films and mobile phone adverts people are always slobbering over each other in arrivals lounges, like the whole time they were away from each other they never doubted the perfection of their reunion for a second. But I was doubting it, big time. I was afraid my OCD would ruin this most momentous day.

I dried myself too fast and scraped my thigh with a fingernail, and took palmfuls of moisturizer and slapped them onto my body. Unlike Nivea Woman, who gently caresses her creamy limbs, inch by inch, quietly congratulating herself on her physical splendour, this is not a job I relish. Many times Toby has stopped me, mid-application, to mimic me – laughing, rubbing his thighs so vigorously that he pushes the air from his lungs, sticking out the tip of his tongue like a toddler with a rattle.

I bronzed my cheeks and put on mascara and applied Vaseline to my cupid's bow to make my lips look fuller. In the mirror I smiled at myself the way I thought I'd smile at him when I saw him, and curved my body into a ridiculous 's', because a straight-on reflection never gives me adequate affirmation before I leave the house that I'm feminine, curvaceous, desirable.

In a taxi I picked at my cuticles and the cracked leather seat. It was 5.50am and in the nearly-dawned sun the salesmen of the town rustled brown paper bags to uncover peanuts and clementines in bicycle baskets. Shop vendors smacked sleeping cows from doorways and mothers washed soapy babies under buckets on the pavements. The air was smoky with fires lit for the first round of chai.

I got out of the taxi at 5.55am. At 6.03am a planeload of people came and went and I couldn't see Toby anywhere, and he wasn't on the next one or the next one either. Every man I saw from a distance had me gripping the handles of my trolley tight.

When he came out of the terminal he couldn't see me at first, but he knew I'd be looking. He knew I'd see his pensive 'where is she?' face and the suggestion of strength in his neck as he turned it. Would he know how I was feeling? Would he know I was feeling *this* good? Maybe not. Thanks to the mood swings that were an inevitable fallout from my secret, decade-long duel between Old Rose and New, he didn't know which Me he was going to get when he knocked on my front door, let alone when he came halfway across the world after six weeks of absence. He was probably just hoping that I'd get through today without crying.

When he finally turned in my direction he broke into a big smile, showing the irregular teeth which made his otherwise immaculate face irresistibly cheeky. I bit my lower lip and grinned as I started to walk towards him, stopping a couple of metres short and readjusting the skirt of my dress, looking down at my feet. On the tarmac his shadow strode towards me and touched me before he did. He put his two hands on either side of my face, tilting it upwards to meet his eyes. We put our brows together and mouthed 'hello' and kissed, first on the lips, then just off the lips, then on the cheeks, the forehead and the eyes. With his hands around my waist he pulled me onto my tiptoes so he could talk into my neck.

'Hello,' he said. I laughed as his stubble tickled my ear.

At the terminal's exit the taxi drivers surrounded us. We agreed a price for a ride to Palolem, one of the most southerly beaches in Goa, and hopped into an old Hindustan Ambassador.

I shuffled up the seat to be next to him, peeling my thighs from the leather upholstery. When the old engine started spluttering I squeezed his knees and limboed under his arm.

My brain was behaving itself startlingly well, but it was still managing to sneak in a few quibbles.

Does his arm feel good around me?

Am I feeling how I thought I'd be feeling?

Is the sunlight from the window exaggerating the blonde down on my thighs?

Relatively, though, the thoughts were docile, sitting viscous at the bottom of this moment beneath a swirling haze of chemicals – lightness, girlishness, giddiness, sex – and didn't show signs of bubbling over just yet.

Breaking from the airport traffic, the taxi careered onto the highway, and in the low morning light we watched Goa rush past the window together for the first time. The countryside was deeply green, possessing volume and depth and drama: big fluffy bushes like giant clumps of moss, next to squat rocket trees and 50-foot palms, like it'd all been whisked up to stand on peaks. Occasionally a bungalow would peep between the palms, painted candy pink or orange or purple or red. Chickens and dogs lay on red clay driveways in the shadows of dusty Honda motorbikes or tuktuks. Women in saris of neon yellow or fuchsia or apricot hung washing and dried chilies and threshed corn. Cows lazed in the road, indifferent to the beeping horns. Just-picked coriander lay in hundreds of baskets by the sides of the roads, its aroma filling the taxi.

I held onto Toby as if he'd disappear if I didn't, and we chatted and kissed, breaking into laughter with each crescendo of the driver's abrasive Bhangra electro. We talked in that jumbled way you do when what you're saying isn't that important, jumping at each other with words like dogs meeting owners at the door.

After an hour of town-peppered jungle we turned onto a narrow, market-fringed road, and squeezed each other's hands to see the sea's blue brilliance at the end of it. A wisp of anxiety licked up my throat as an image of the topless sunbathers who might be waiting there darted into my mind.

What the hell will Toby think if I trigger on the beach?
How will I hide the trembles?

We paid the taxi driver and stepped onto the hot sand of Palolem. It was the first time Toby had been anywhere tropical, and I pulled his arm and pointed and jabbered at him, too-eager, like I was showing the new kid around school.

Trained to spot the craning shapes of backpackers from a distance – beetles on hind legs – the hut owners were on the beach within seconds, asking us where we were staying and promising 'good price' and 'good room'. We chose a collection of six huts 20 metres back from the beach, shaded by a grove of giant palms, with hammocks hanging between them.

We stepped blinking into the hut and my nerves fluttered in my chest as the image of a greasy row of oiled tits flashed up against the double bed's white sheets.

Through the lattice shutters the sun shone. A white muslin net hung from the ceiling and draped over the mattress, creating a milky cube of light in the middle of the room. We got inside. He turned to kiss me and I pressed my hand against him, feeling his chest rise and fall under his shirt. His head smelt warm from where the sun had hit the pillow. We lay there for a few minutes, watching the palm shadows dapple one timber wall, and in their flickering midst that image flashed up once more.

It's going to ruin it.

But as Toby moved his hands across the dimples of my back, each of my thoughts were present and easy like molasses and I didn't even notice that I was thinking. Kissing him now, I was away from my mind and away from that place, unselfconscious and content, a quintessence of nothingness. I wasn't in India on a palm-fringed beach, I was unthinkingly in love on that sun-warm bed. And there, with the noon light dappling the feather-delicate muslin all around us, I glimpsed the Me that might be.

Viennetta

Pure O. Pure as the driven snow. Pure poetry. Pure and simple, etcetera, etcetera. Needless to say I don't feel too 'pure' when I've awoken every morning for a fortnight to the crystalline thought of assholes. Seriously, assholes before breakfast every day are a singularly depressing phenomenon, and they've never kept the doctor away, I can tell you.

But what the hell is it? And how is it obsessive compulsive disorder? And how do I have it?

Well, contrary to what many people think, OCD doesn't have anything to do with cleanliness or neatness. OCD is a disorder characterised by excessive doubt about a specific theme or specific themes. That theme *may* be something like cleanliness or neatness – a person with OCD might have obsessive doubts about the contamination of a table top, for example – but obsessive doubt can fixate on pretty much anything: whether or not you're straight, whether or not you're gay, whether or not your house will fall down, whether or not you're going to hell, whether or not you want to cheat on your spouse, whether or not you're a latent arsonist, whether or not you're actually *alive*, etcetera. The list goes on. Whatever the themes of the 'doubting disease', as OCD is also known, the same mechanism of indefatigable uncertainty remains.

OCD isn't just a vague ball of neurotic repetitive behaviour, either. It's made up of two very distinct symptoms: obsessions and compulsions. Obsessions are unwanted distressing thoughts, doubts or mental images which cause anxiety; compulsions are any attempt to neutralise, solve or escape them. So, just as someone with a contamination obsession might try to neutralise a doubt about spreading germs by carrying out a cleaning compulsion, an obsessive with a homicide obsession might try to neutralise a doubt about killing people by silently telling themselves they're a good person. The latter is an example of the fabled 'pure O', so nicknamed because the compulsions are very subtle. To the untrained eye the disorder looks like a 'purely obsessional' version of OCD.

The rationale is fair enough, I guess, but whoever came up with that name must have been a fucking comedian. What was the thought process? Were they sat round in the boardroom trying to decide on a name for this wracked-off neurosis that no-one ever really talked about? Was there a jaded senior Namer there, a relic from the pre-acronym glory days when illnesses were oozing with Latinate poeticism and names like Diphtheria and Variola and Pyrexia abounded, when old-school Namers like him were still respected creatives plying their craft, and suggestions like MRSA or AIDS would've been laughed out of the building for their sheer ugliness? In his resentment and ennui did he now entertain himself day to day with the blackly ironic baptism of every neurosis that landed on his desk? Did he stub out his cigarette and thump his fist on the table with mock-excitement and say, 'I've got it, goddammit. I've got it'? Did he lean back on his chair, clasp one palm to his bosom and sweep the other across the middle distance with

a Judy Garland smile and say, 'This rape-y, murder-y, pae-
do-y disorder ... Let's call it *Pure* ...'?

Contrary to its media portrayal, OCD is not the mental
busywork of coddled Westerners; it affects people from all
socioeconomic backgrounds, all over the world. Nor is it a
'new' disorder brought about by modern societal shifts.
History is littered with examples of OCD traits, which were
often chalked up to 'religious melancholy'. In 1691, Bishop
John Moore gave a sermon in London's Whitehall to a con-
gregation including Queen Mary II. In it, he described
'unhappy persons, who have naughty, and sometimes Blasphemous Thoughts start in their Minds ... Christians,
whom these bad Thoughts so vex and torment, [despite] all
their endeavours to stifle and suppress them. Nay, often the
more they struggle with them, the more they encrease'.

The exact cause of OCD is not known. Biological,
environmental and genetic factors are all thought to
contribute. For many years now, scientists have been
investigating whether a serotonin imbalance could be at the
root of obsessive compulsive symptoms, or whether their
onset could be the result of antibodies released in response
to ear, nose and throat infections. These antibodies may
interfere with functioning in the basal ganglia, an area of the
brain associated with obsessive compulsive activity. More
recent studies are exploring whether abnormally high levels
of the neurotransmitter glutamate could lead to neuron
damage, and so to OCD, or whether elevated levels of the
hormone oxytocin – a chemical associated with intimacy,
pair-bonding and sex – could be to blame.

It's difficult to know how many people are out there right

now choking down their Viennettas over some unpalatable OCD thought. One estimate suggests that 1% of the global population has 'pure O' – that's 630,000 in the UK alone – but it could be much higher, as many people with the condition don't even realise that they've got it. Why would they? If a teenage girl was suddenly seized by a graphic, paedophilic thought, and she had no knowledge of the world or of mental health, and every day the telly was glorying in sensational tales about impossible evils wrought on small bodies in basements, why would she *not* assume she was guilty?

Or if a teenage boy was suddenly seized by repetitive thoughts about manually shagging his sister with, say, the narrow end of an avocado, why would he assume that he had a neurotic disorder? How could he possibly know that messages were misfiring in his brain and preventing him from dismissing the kind of what-the-fuck doubts that most people shrug off without worry? He couldn't. He'd assume that he had a deep-rooted personal problem which needed resolving.

In an effort to do so, he might curl up with his laptop, shaking, and start Googling the meaning behind his thoughts. He might deliberately conjure mental images of his sister while monitoring how he felt: aroused or repulsed? Excited or horrified? To avoid anxiety-prompting scenarios he might start ignoring her calls and skipping family mealtimes. He might vow to avoid guacamole forever. He might spend ten, sixteen, twenty hours a day in a secret spiral of rumination and problem solving, trying to figure out what the *hell* was happening to him.

And he wouldn't understand this yet, but all these behaviours would merely be compulsions – the tell-tale signs of his chronic anxiety disorder. And the signs would go unread, because unlike with a contamination obsession, where irrational cleaning compulsions would make his mental condition patently obvious to those around him, his behaviour would be inside his head, or behind closed doors. And because he was so terrified of someone discovering his shameful obsession with incest (and avocados) he'd strive for normality, outwardly smiling through the worst of his thoughts.

What if you were a mother and you kept having doubts about drowning your baby in the bath? How would you talk about it then? Or an old woman who kept imagining flashing the vicar? Or a gay man who kept having thoughts about tits when he made love to his husband? You'd keep it secret for years; for your whole life, perhaps. You'd be an anonymous blog post or a journal hidden under the bed, and even though you had what the World Health Organization considers one of the ten most debilitating disorder, in the world, not a soul would know.

This understanding has filtered through me over the years like water through rock. But back in my uni room that night, with the Chuck Taylors whipping on the telephone line, it was a wall of new knowledge and it smashed me like a sea wave, and *Ten Years Younger* was well into its second ad break by the time I was able to pull myself off the carpet.

I began to pace. 'Shit shit shit,' I said, draining my cigarette. This was it – *the answer.* The proof of my identity. In my chest a disco ball as big as the world sent a billion sparkles spinning. *I HAVE A DIAGNOSIS.*

I was so happy I lost control of my body for a few minutes

or hours, punching the mattress and getting all tangled up in the curtains and eating pillow cases and such. The Incredible Hulk on Christmas morning. I'd changed species. Metamorphosed. I was not the same person anymore. Knowledge is power and with my new power I could do anything.

The story of my life had changed and that night I rewatched it a thousand times, with the director's commentary turned on this time, trembling and laughing and shaking my head. *Of course. Of course. Of motherfucking course.* My self made sense for the first time. I had my Me back. I had never been a paedophile – I had never 'sinned in my thoughts', and I'd never been through a sexual identity crisis, I was just *ill*. Half a life of uncertainty and now this: the end.

Obsessions and compulsions. Obsessions and compulsions. Obsessions and compulsions. So my obsession was my sexual identity, and all those hours I'd spent deliberately scouring my memory for evidence of my sexuality had been compulsions.

Wow.

Wow.

Wow.

All the times I'd interrogated the sexual play of my childhood – Barbie and Ken and Kiss The Bride: compulsions. Trying to convince myself that I was gay; trying to convince myself that I was straight: compulsions. *Diva* and *Attitude* and the lap dance and Cherie and Tony: all compulsions, all irresistible rituals, all answer-seeking checks, all howlingly symptomatic of a serious mental condition I never knew I had—

—But, WAIT. I stopped dead in the centre of my room.

What about Rachel? Had even that been a compulsive act? *Surely* if I was a straight person with OCD and not a closeted gay person, I would never have done that?

NO! Already: a new doubt lacerating my newfound sense of finality, morphing me back into what I was before. I had to find an answer, RIGHT NOW. I had to get confirmation that Titgate had come within the remit of compulsive behaviour, ironically not recognising that in doing so I was merely engaging in yet another answer-seeking compulsion.

I sat down at my desk again and started hacking away at the keyboard, Googling phrases like 'OCD compulsions', 'pure O rituals' and 'sexual experimentation OCD'. My anxiety soared. This new question once again threatened who I was, and if I couldn't find a factual and scientific answer my world would fall apart once more.

Click-click.

'Compulsive sexual experimentation is sometimes engaged in by people with very severe obsessive compulsive sexual orientation doubts.'

Oh thank fuck.

'In some rare cases persons have actually engaged in homosexual behaviour to find a resolution to complete the search. These people think that if they find the encounter stimulating, then they are gay. On the other hand, if they are turned off by the encounter they feel they can rest assured they are straight.'

Oh my God, that's EXACTLY it.

'It is within this desperate effort that deeper levels of ambiguity are delivered as a payback for the OCD sufferer's desperate search. The age-old adage, "the more we learn, the more questions we have" is certainly relevant here.'

My breathing slowed. Delectable clarity as a calmness washed over my brain, my sense of self once more restored. I raced my eyes back down the Google search page to see if any more useful info could be gleaned. The phrase 'body scanning' jumped out at me.

Click-click.

'The person with sexual orientation OCD may check for signs of sexual arousal when near people of the opposite sex to ensure continued heterosexuality, or check for signs of non-arousal with people of the same sex to ensure he hasn't become gay.'

Wow – that explained Debbie Does Dudley – that night when I'd tried to read my body for signs while staring at him. (And in years to come it would also explain why, when a drunk, wrinkly German flopped out her moggy, un-announced, and soaked the scorched Oktoberfest grass with her piss, I'd stand there rigid with fear, silently nursing a fatty in my pants.)

I clicked to another page: 'If a sufferer were to see an attractive person of the same sex and check whether they are having a completely neutral sensation in their groin, there is a significant likelihood that they would feel a tingling and miss out on the opportunity to disqualify their homosexual inclination.'

This was life-changing stuff. I couldn't keep up. I tore a piece of paper from a note pad and wrote down two crucial new bits of info, lest I forgot them (once again not realising that I was acting out a toxic compulsion): 'All my arousal-like sensations when looking at women have been a symptom of OCD. And so was my attempt at sexual experimentation.' I read the sentence again and again and again, 20 times, 50 times, rolling my shoulders, boxing the air, 80 times, 100 times, hopping from foot to foot and reading it out loud making sure it was really, really, really cemented in my mind—

—But wait. 'WAIT,' I said, putting down my pen and screwing the paper in my fist, as a new, harrowing possibility crossed my mind: if sexual experimentation can be used compulsively by people obsessed with whether or not they might be gay, can it also be used compulsively by people obsessed with whether or not they might be paedophiles?

Oh fuck, no. Did I have a condition which counted THAT as one of its legitimate symptoms? *I feel sick.* It was too awful. Too evil. This is why I never told anyone about this stuff. It was just too fucked up. *I've got to know I've got to know I've got to know.* I took to Google once more, trying to find an answer, crying buckets.

Click click.

'Compulsive "acting out" of an obsessive fear is peculiar to people with sexual orientation obsessions, as, unlike with many other themes, the behaviour is not generally seen by the sufferer as morally transgressive.'

Oh, thank fuck.

'There's no-one I'd trust more to babysit my kids than someone with paedophilic OCD thoughts,' a doctor had written, 'they'd go to the greatest lengths to avoid doing them harm.'

To steady myself I gripped the desk edge with two hands and rested my forehead on top of them, blinking heavy droplets and watching them curve to the floor and land beside my toes. The foot bay of the desk was a cube of warm and dark light, like a den me and Patty would've made, and

I felt like getting inside. I sat curled in a ball for I don't know how long, contemplating the hugeness of the things I'd just read, contemplating how they might change my life for the better. Now I had a diagnosis I'd be able to answer every doubt with an irrefutable fact: 'I know who I am.'

Beach Bodies

The following morning I strode through the Leeds campus, swinging my arms and singing 'La Bamba' into the wind. I felt like I had a whole team of muscle around me, a protective scrum, and my thoughts – my *obsessions*, they had a name now! – were simply too puny to contend with our might. Pretty girls, adverts, club flyers: the usual triggers could not contend with me now. I had unlocked the secret to my Self.

'BAAAAA-BA-BAMBA . . .'

After several days I knew whole sections of several OCD articles by heart, so that when my doubts arose it didn't matter – my arsenal of knowledge was too strong.

After about a week I was at the Student Union buying a Chomp. I walked to the till along the magazine aisle, where I had many times stopped to act out compulsive checks: flitting my eyes a hundred times between the suits on the men's mags and the bikinis on the women's mags. But I felt confident this time, and breezed towards the checkout, drinking in those covers, immune—

Halfway down I stopped like a yanked dog to see 'BEACH BODIES!' on a gossip mag. A woman with massive tits sunbathing on the beach. A lump shot to my throat and the doubts came in a split-second flurry:

Why did I notice her?

What if I'm not really ill?

What if these thoughts are *the truth?*

What if I'm lying to myself?

This assault was unexpected given my newfound confidence, but it was fine. It would *all* be fine. Because now I had weapons to deploy:

'I know who I am. I have OCD. I know who I am,' I whispered, standing still in the aisle and staring hard at the pink triangles of Lycra, trying not to imagine what they concealed. But still the doubts fired:

Maybe the fact I noticed her means I'm gay?

No. I have OCD. I know who I am.

But if I did have OCD surely I wouldn't question it?

So, maybe I'm gay?

No. I know who I am.

And the spiral continued as I shuffled back home across campus, back through the dark wet park, singing nothing, with the unopened Chomp withering in my fist.

Pretty much everyone gets intrusive thoughts. All sorts of weird shit that you don't tell anyone about – those thoughts that feel alien and un-You and seem to come from nowhere. Like when you imagine punching your smiling hairdresser in the throat, or slapping a bald man's head, or jumping off a train platform. *Do I really want to do THAT?*, you think.

Or when you have those bizarre if-I-did-X-then-Y-would-happen thoughts: if I dropped this baby, it'd die; if I defecated on this carpet I'd get fired; if I stood behind that woman and laid my willy down the bridge of her nose like a Corinthian helmet . . . And so forth.

Through a questionnaire presented to a group of healthy students, psychologist Stanley Rachman found that virtually all of them had such thoughts occasionally, including thoughts of sexual violence, blasphemous or obscene mental images, thoughts of harming elderly people, violence against animals or towards children, and impulsive or abusive outbursts or utterances.

But the problem doesn't lie in the thoughts themselves – they're just part of the human mind's unfathomable weirdness – the problem lies in the way that people with OCD respond to them. You see, there's something going on in their brains, some little neurotic fizz or glitch, which prevents them from dismissing the anomalous thoughts that most people shrug off without worry. The thoughts then get stuck like a broken record, and in their maddening repetitiveness, they start to feel like legitimate concerns, becoming a catastrophic challenge to the deepest facets of the person's identity. Every little thought about stabbing a loved one becomes concrete evidence of a real life homicidal tendency, and no matter how many compulsions they enact, the doubt would never be dispelled.

So there was nothing unusual about my having imagined the BEACH BODIES woman naked. We've all been there. What was unusual was my inability to dismiss that image, and my urgent need to analyse it for meaning, and my inability to be satisfied with the fruits of that analysis. And my subsequent compulsive urge to go straight back online that night and read the same articles I'd already read, to recite the same mantras which had so often failed, to look at the same nude-y pics that I already knew pixel by pixel by pixel.

*

Back then I didn't know that these repetitive behaviours were only fuelling my doubts. Back then I didn't know *shit*, except that, as the weeks wore on, and I researched more and more, I was becoming increasingly convinced that I had OCD. But how could I be sure? How could I be 100% unequivocally positive? I needed to explain my self-diagnosis – as unbelievable as it sounded – to another human for the first time.

Clipart

A new doctor, a new consulting room, and a new set of questions.

'Were you abused as a child?'

'No.'

'You're sure?'

'Yes.

'And you don't think you could be bottling up a memory of something traumatic like that?'

'No.'

'Because, you know, these things often manifest in our present internal experience.'

'Okay.'

She types something into the computer. 'And you mentioned you have thoughts about being gay?'

'Yes.'

'And you think that's shameful?'

'No! God, no . . .' *She thinks I'm a phobe.* I swallowed hard. 'Absolutely not. *Of course* there's nothing wrong with being gay. I'd much rather be gay than this. I just can't shake off the doubt. I can't stand not knowing whether I am or not, and I know it sounds weird but I really don't feel like I am.'

'Mmm hmmm,' she said, raising an eyebrow. *She doesn't believe me. Why would she? I barely believe myself.* 'What's your relationship like with your—'

'—Erm, I'm really sorry, I don't mean to interrupt, but . . . like I've said, I really think, from what I've read, that I might have obsessive compulsive disorder or something. It's the only thing that's ever kind of made sense.'

'Thank you, Rose, I've made a note of that, and I'll make sure the therapist is aware of it.' Kind. Dismissive. 'You mentioned that in your early adolescence you sometimes faked feeling unwell. Can you remember why that was?'

Panic rising in my chest. If she wasn't getting it, maybe I'd misdiagnosed myself. Maybe she was right to ignore the OCD thing. Maybe I *didn't* know who I was after all.

I left the room and slid along the surgery's magnolia corridor walls. A navy blue flyer was thumb-tacked to a noticeboard: 'When blue is your primary colour' typed above a clipart guy with a cloud raining on his bowed head – ironically the most depressing piece of design on campus. Next to it a red poster: 'Keep calm and end stigma'. Someone had turned the dot of the 'i' into a smiley face, and it was all so pathetic, all so telling of underpaid mental health staff with a blitzkrieg spirit working alone on 10-year-old computers under foam ceiling tiles. It made me cry.

Soon I got a letter telling me that I was going to have 20 hours of 'psychodynamic therapy', and that I had to wait two months for my first session. I Googled it at once: 'a form of depth psychology, the primary focus of which is to reveal the unconscious content of a client's psyche in an effort to alleviate psychic tension.' 'Depth': that's what I needed. *Finally*, someone would explore my depths and tell me who I was.

*

Fast forward to my first session, and me giving the same explanation I'd given to the GP, the same explanation I'd give to umpteen docs in the future:

'I keep having thoughts that I might be gay,' I said, 'and I've tried to tell myself that I need to accept that I am, but I just can't *get there* with my feelings, if you know what I mean? It just doesn't feel like *me*.'

'Well, let's ask ourselves a question, Rose: what if you *were* gay?' she said, smiling, like a schoolteacher. 'What if?'

'That'd be okay,' I said in a small voice.

'Well then,' she said, as if we'd just made a breakthrough, 'that's what you need to tell yourself when the thoughts come: it's okay. To. Be. You.' I'd told *myself* that a million times already, but it sounded different coming from her.

She was calm and assertive as she explained what was to come. The two of us would build a close 'interpersonal relationship' which would help me relate to others. We would work together to create a list of all the reasons my doubts were irrational. We would explore why I found an OCD diagnosis 'helpful'. And we would talk about *why* it was okay to be whoever I wanted to be in a 'safe and trusting environment'. It was all so cosy.

By the second session we were exploring the events of my past in an attempt to explain my present anxieties. I told her about some of the memories that made me anxious: Kiss The Bride and the Sextaurant and Fart FM (ever tried telling a stranger that as a kid you were mad for ass?) – and she said I had to keep telling myself that there was nothing to be ashamed of. I nodded and wept, confused. I didn't think I *was* objectively ashamed of these things. I was just crazy with doubts about what they meant. But if *she* thought that my distress was caused by the shameful suppression of sexual memories, then it must have been. She was the expert.

After 20 sessions the course was finished, and it was also graduation time. Psychodynamic therapy had taught me that it was okay to be whoever I wanted to be – gay, straight, bi, *whatever* – I deserved happiness and I didn't need labels like 'OCD' to get it. I just had to think positive. I felt the momentousness and the supposed-to of an impending New Chapter: leaving university and blossoming into a successful, measured adult. So I left Leeds, hell bent on forging a new, mature Me. London was calling.

Kate Moss

The wheels of the golf buggy skidded on the perfect lawn. It was very late. My colleague Harry and I were scream-ing-laughing and gurning our tits off as we speeded through the dark, veering around stone lions set on plinths and topi-aried rose bushes. It'd been a long day: Michelin star five course lunch, followed by falconry, followed by Michelin star banquet, followed by croquet, followed by drinks in the drawing room, followed by 'a turn on the lawn' which we'd spiced up with a baggie or two. We'd got drunk at the earliest opportunity, of course: champagne with the morel and pea-foam starter at midday, and eked through the rest of the formalities creasing to watch each other feigning interest in the odious tales of PR bore after PR bore. At midnight, we asked the maître-d' for a bacon 'n' brown sauce sarnie and watched as his stoic sycophancy finally crumbled into dis-dain. We could barely stand for laughing.

Harry – our publication's arts and culture editor – was our best blagger, but by his own admission this was the most wonderful and disgraceful freebie he'd ever blagged: an all-expenses-paid luxury weekend at the five star Branley Hall resort in the lush burbs of London. *THIS is what's possible when you're a journalist in the BIG CITY,* I thought.

*

Objectively I was loving my new life. I'd moved down here straight off the back of my first round-the-world trip, which I'd saved for by working in a bank after graduating. I'd spent three months travelling the well-trod route through Thailand, Malaysia, Singapore, Australia, New Zealand, Fiji and Los Angeles, drinking every day to stave off the reality of my doubts, which had by then been with me for eight years: 3000 days.

The trip had been notable for two instances.

The first happened at the infamous Full Moon Party on the island Koh Pangnan in Thailand, to which successive generations, unswayed by Alex Garland's visceral tales of paradise lost, come searching for partying's zenith. It's held on Haad Rin beach: half a mile of tribal tattoos and panama hats and glowsticks, fluorescent bikinis, Kate Moss T-shirts and Billabong. Here people drink out of buckets instead of glasses and shag up the trunks of trees where birds used to roost. 'Sex on Fire' plays five times a night. In my pocket were two brown capsules which a local man had hawked me on the promise they'd show me a good time. 'Take half,' he'd said, 'only half.'

Later, on the beach, a voice behind me: 'Can I buy you a drink?' I heard but pretended not to, because with a sinking heart I knew it belonged to the guy I'd just seen pissing into the sea. 'Oi, can I buy you a drink?' he said again, louder. I turned round to look at him and his weasely little mate. He was swaying and squinting at the fading sun and his fattish body was badly burnt. White globs of saliva had gathered in the corners of his skinny mouth, evoking a memory in my flesh of all those bad-breath, bad-shoes boys who leant up against you in Black Country Lloyds Bars, reeking of fags and sambuca. I said 'no thank you' and turned my back to him.

'Ah, we thought you were a dyke, anyway,' he said. And they walked away laughing.

I pulled the capsules out of my pocket. With the humidity and body heat they'd welded together and there was no way of halving them, so I did the whole gooey lot, and woke up alone in my bed the following night, not knowing what day it was, or why I did the things I did, or whether or not there'd been any truth in what that boy had said, or how, after therapy, I could still feel *this* fucked.

The second notable instance happened on a beach on the north of the island. It was full of stoner ex-pats – Garland's generation – who resented the south side's teenyboppers and their Black Eyed Peas, and it was much calmer here, though the weather was stormy.

At the headland bar one night I found myself helplessly ruminating about a beautiful Kiwi girl who was drinking at the next table.

Do I fancy her?
Do I fancy her?
Do I fancy her?

Then later, on the beach by the fire, she lay down next to me, giggling, and put her hand on mine and squeezed it. I turned to face her, and she had on this sexy little smile, and it made me weird right down to my toes, and I snatched my hand away and ran up the sand into the darkness under the palms. In my hut I sat rocking in a square of moonlight for an hour, wondering whether I did the right thing, wondering whether I'd have enjoyed it if I'd tried it, wondering if my doubts were OCD or reality, wondering who I found more attractive: the fat 'you're a dyke' guy or the beautiful Kiwi girl, wondering whether to go after her or to stay here, paralysed by indecision.

More than anything I was ashamed. My behaviour must have appeared so uptight and so terribly illiberal. Before all these thoughts had started, I'd been burgeoning into someone who was open-minded and pro-sex and pro-bodies. Gleefully, I'd begun to kick back against my Catholic education and question my RE teachers about the arbitrariness of their doctrines. I'd wanted to be a warrior of free inquiry, and nothing had maddened me more than rules for the sake of rules. And yet here I was now: my own tyrant, enforcing nonsensical rules upon *myself,* rules I did not understand but could not flout, repressing myself and inhibiting myself. If I could've stepped into a lesbian identity and taken away the searing uncertainty, I'd have done it in a heartbeat, but I could not – I didn't understand why but I simply *could not.* There was nothing 'free' about it. No glimmer of the grown-up I'd once wanted to become.

But years later I would come to realise something that would go some way towards assuaging my shame. I am, after all, in a unique position for a straight person, in that I've spent large swathes of my life irrationally trying *everything* within my power to convince my brain that I'm gay. And the fact that I could not, no matter how much I tried, sticks a triumphant middle finger up to anyone who dares to suggest that homosexuality is not something innate and therefore deserving of respect, but a *choice*, a choice consciously made in perversion of God or The Family or whatever the hell else. Believe me, if it was a choice I would have made it. It doesn't work like that. I've tried.

I've tried and tried and tried.

Now here I was in London, still brown from three drunken months in the sun, sleeping on friends' sofas and interning on the dance music section of an events guide, going to gigs and festivals and restaurants and gallery openings – wringing First Thursdays for every drop of arty booze. All for free. On paper it was a dream, and it felt like a dream, too. The gap between waking and dream states, sober and drunk, private and public, had never been wider. On Facebook I was louche and carefree, pouting and dressing up and dancing. In reality I was sober and lonely and mental.

Town & Country

After about a year of living in London I'd found myself a room in a flat – above the launderette on the estate in Shoreditch, where the two fat titty women always smoked outside – and an actual paid editorial job. The doubts were grinding on and spectacularly violating my hopes of transformation, and at work I was regularly breaking down in the toilets at lunchtime. But somehow I was still optimistic, because now I was in London, dreamcity, where I could surely access world-class psychiatric care.

The NHS waiting lists were predictably long, but I was earning now, so I decided to go private. This was not something anyone in my family *ever* did (except in the most extreme 'life threatening' cases – like when Mom and Dad gave me a CAT scan for my faked illness all those years ago) so I had come to associate 'going private' with the best service available, the crème de la crème de la crème. I found a BABCP-accredited cognitive behavioural therapist who charged £95 an hour. I figured anyone asking for that much must be the best there is. And the website looked proper fancy, too.

The day of my first session came.

I walked up the woodchip hall of an old London mansion block and into the waiting room. Same rough carpet, same water cooler, same old copies of *Town & Country*, same jittery strangers chewing the rims of plastic cups that I'd seen in every underfunded NHS clinic I'd ever been to. What had I been expecting? A Buck's Fizz welcome drink? A mariachi band? I don't know. But it didn't feel very 'private'.

I knocked on door 3.

'Hello,' said a cheerful voice.

'Hi.' I went in. The therapist was in her mid forties with scruffy red hair – 'a bit of a hippie' as she later described herself. She invited me to sit and asked me how I was feeling with a big smile.

'So you're having some pesky obsessive-compulsive thoughts, are you?'

'Well, the last therapist didn't think I had OCD.'

'I've seen your assessment, dear, there's absolutely *no* doubt.'

'My last therapist thought I was just looking for a label.'

'Well, between you and me,' she said, leaning forward, smiling, 'your last therapist was a little off the mark. We can do better than that.' She winked.

I adored her immediately.

She explained that therapy would use an evidence-based approach to rationalise my thinking distortions and help me build a 'New Rose'. New Rose would enjoy people's company. New Rose would pay people compliments. New Rose would be brave. New Rose would hug people spontaneously and eat well and not drink too much. New Rose wouldn't let Old Rose's pesky negative thoughts overwhelm her. New Rose would be positive and confident. New Rose had to write a manifesto, and live by it:

'If I tell someone I am genuinely happy for them and genuinely feel happy for them, then I will feel good and make them feel good.

If I hug a friend spontaneously I will feel a friendly, bonding experience.

If I accept that being aroused by women doesn't make me gay, then I can enjoy arousal without it making me anxious.

If I engage people in conversation then I will feel more confident and enjoy interaction.

If I talk to people about my OCD then people will accept me and I will feel more understood.'

It all sounded so perfect. This was who I wanted to be. Sociable, confident, happy. And for months and months I devoted every waking moment to putting my manifesto into action, believing all the way to the bottom of my heart that this was the *key* to finally forging a clear-cut identity.

'You'll get there,' the therapist said one difficult session towards the end of the course. 'Keep practising New Rose and you'll get there.'

'I am, I promise,' I said, fretting, 'but I still have all these doubts—'

'Listen, Rose, I'm going to tell you something now that I don't usually tell my other clients . . .'

'Okay.'

'. . . I'm gay—' A bolt of terror in my chest. *Maybe I've*

insulted her. *Maybe she thinks I'm a phobe.* '—and I know, from speaking to you, that you're just *not gay.* There's no way. Your experience is *not* the experience of a gay person, you have *OCD*. Trust me, I know. So stop worrying about it.'

'Seriously?' I said, crying.

'Yeessss! Absolutely. Girls *never* made me anxious like they make you feel anxious. Anxiety is diametrically opposite to arousal – you need to keep reminding yourself that.'

I almost danced down the woodchip hallway, toot-toot-tooting like Steamboat Willie past the ghastly faces in the waiting room. 'That's it, that's it, that's it,' I whispered. It was the first time anyone has ever spelt out an answer to me – AN ANSWER – emphatically and categorically: this is who you are. It was a professional opinion! *That's it.*

But just a day later that certainty had already crumbled and I was anxious once more. I'd put *all* my strength into trying to block out my negative old self and usher in a new one – but it only seemed to have fed directly back into my obsessive doubts:

If I really had OCD, therapy would work.

So maybe I'm gay.

But obsessive doubting is a symptom of OCD, so therapy is the right thing to do.

But therapy isn't working.

If I really had OCD, therapy would work.

After a week of spiralling like this I emailed the therapist:

'Despite practising New Rose very hard, and having become much more mindful of when I'm obsessing, I have been feeling extremely anxious, and have ruminated for 12 hours a day most days. This is the worst I have felt since starting therapy. I've thought about wanting to die on many occasions since our last session and have started cutting myself again. I can't eat much because food isn't going down well and I'm losing weight as a result. I've been skipping work and I've started physically twitching in response to unwanted thoughts. I seem to trigger at the slightest thing now. Any exposed flesh whatsoever makes me question my arousal levels. I worry that if therapy isn't making me better then maybe I should just accept that I can't be happy in a relationship with a man because it's with a person of the wrong sex . . . The obsessions are more unrelenting and frightening than ever. I'm reaching a point of despair as I don't feel like the current method is working, and I'm not sure what I should do next.'

And she replied:

'Now it seems like "old" Rose is still fighting back, as you describe the anxiety as still being with you. Are you still practising your relaxation breathing exercises each day? Also, you need to eat three meals a day and keep your sleep pattern as stable as you can, as all these things will lower your mood and make you feel anxious . . . As for the anxiety, try writing a story of the very first time you ever felt anxious and what happened to you. Well done for all the work and progress you have made and don't let "old" Rose win now that you are so close to changing things around in your life.'

*

It was a Catch 22, rank and absurd. My Old Rose negativity merely served to prove how much I needed to work on New Rose. My belief that therapy was flawed was actually *proof* of therapy's credence. There was something so dogmatic and oppressive about it, and I couldn't quite put my finger on why it upset me so much, but it gave me the same feeling of feeble outrage that I'd felt as a little kid when the RE teacher had said that the painful doubts of the faithful actually *prove* the existence of God, since their suffering brings them closer to Jesus. I'd screwed up my tiny fists with frustration – how could grown-ups say these things?

Though my therapist was lovely and she meant well, and had doubtless entered psychiatry with a hope of helping people, her approach was based on a sort of benign intellectual bullying – and it had the ironically un-therapeutic effect of heightening my sense of failure, driving me further and further away from the new, confident Me that therapy was supposed to unveil.

Coke and Champagne

When I woke up at an hour later in the Goan heat, I was dazed and forgetful for a couple of seconds, but when I saw Toby lying next to me, I let out an involuntary 'oh' and put my arms around him and kissed the back of his neck.

We wandered down to the sea, playing hopscotch around the cow pats in the sand, watching the tiny crabs disappear into holes in the glittering shallows as we passed. We held hands as we climbed to a café on the headland, and had watermelon juice and Nutella on toast.

'Lennie!' Toby said, pointing at the juice I'd spilled on the table and the Nutella in my hair. He called me that whenever I did something clumsy, which happened most days, after Lennie in *Of Mice and Men*, who accidentally squashes his puppy in his pocket with too-affectionate strokes.

'You loved it too much, didn't you?' Toby said, wiping the Nutella from my hair with a napkin.

The next days dizzied by. We swam and boozed and sunbathed. We drank madeira on the wooden porch, listened to the crickets, watched the clouds roll over the tropical moon. The doubts were there, but they were looser and softer, somehow – they didn't linger as long. I was blustering at the end of the branch, fragile and papery, but for now, high. Perhaps being here with him was curing me. Perhaps all my efforts were finally paying off. Perhaps therapy actually *had* worked and I really was transforming. Perhaps, after all my scepticism, New Rose could be happy with a man because she'd chosen to *believe* in happiness, because she was finally thinking positively.

In fantastic little beachside restaurants with neon signs and fairy-lit palm trunks, we ate like kings. Three courses, five courses, seven courses. At Brendan's, a beachside restaurant – and according to its sign, a 'Very Cool Place' – I ordered a 'Brendan's Special Desserts', because it entertained us to gamble on cryptic menu items.

'If it's a big one you'll have to help me with it,' I said, rubbing my palms together between my knees. 'I don't know if I'll fit it in.'

'But what about the *dessert*?' Toby asked, spluttering into his 'Brendan's Special Cocktails'.

It arrived. Digestive biscuits, tinned peaches, whipped cream: spectacular.

A 'hmphf' sound as a mangy dog flumped at Toby's feet, tail aloft, presenting its puckered asshole towards our table. We groaned and doubled up laughing, mouths full of cream, and Toby shuffled a mound of sand to cover the offending hoop.

That night, walking tipsily along the broken tarmac through the orange streetlight and the shadows of the palm fronds, a fantastical sense of a beautiful, dystopian future washed over us. Now we were wandering through a country in the aftermath of a hot disaster. The electricity pylons all rusted and leaning, with a thousand threadbare wires spewing in every direction. Singed plastic bags draped amid their coils.

Fey moths flapping against the lights. The forever-open shops with corrugated iron sides and blue tarp roofs, selling half-empty suncream and outdated maps. Above the sound of the spluttering generators we heard the steaming sound of cow piss and saw a stray dog skulkily licking it from the pavement before trotting off into the ever-encroaching undergrowth, which was always advancing and reclaiming, stronger than concrete. Vines choking lamp posts, roots crumbling walls.

The next day we hired a scooter and rode into the hills and saw macaws and monkeys. I ruminated briefly on my mind's new, dominant question as to whether I liked the feeling of Toby's arms around my waist as I rode the bike, and whether or not I'd prefer the touch of a woman. But those unfettered moments in the hut on the first day had strengthened my resolve to banish my doubts, and after a few minutes' intense rationalisation – *of COURSE I like his touch* – the question subsided. We reached the top of the mountainous jungle and watched its miles and miles of emerald roll into the deep, Arabian sea.

After a week we left Palolem and went south to Rajbag beach, where we rented a room in a charming fuchsia colonial building. In its back yard lived a skittish, puppy-like pig with whom Toby developed a game of peep-o.

The young pig would see him approach and skip away to the back of its pen, then Toby would crouch down with just his head peering over the breezeblock wall, which separated man and beast. The pig would edge back towards him, pretending not to look at him. Then, when it was very close to the other side of the wall, poised just like a dog waiting for a stick to be thrown, Toby would suddenly rise up and grunt loudly, and the pig would tear off to the back of the pen, squealing with delight, and Toby would crouch back down, giggling irrepressibly until the game started again.

On the far side of the pig's dusty enclosure was a high rhododendron hedge, and beyond that were the manicured lawns of the Goa Intercontinental hotel. Toby and I peeked through the leaves at the orchid-spotted gardens then turned to face each other, grinning.

'Shall we?'

Neither of us could afford a place as fancy as that, but we could pretend. Wearing our smartest clothes we strode confidently up the sweeping driveway and into the grand marble lobby, smiling at the staff, and without dithering, strolled through to the terrace and looked out over the pristine golf course towards the beach, as though all of it was ours. Sauntering on through the rose garden I smelt the unmistakable smell of chlorine and a slow, forceful anxiety rose in my chest as I imagined bikinis and glistening skin. But when we turned the corner, the pool was empty and I relaxed.

We walked on, marvelling at each new little luxury – the Jacuzzis and the in-pool cocktail bars and the massage tables and the twinkling underwater lights. The sun had started to set and turn the water pink. We stood on a little bridge over the pool, holding hands.

'One day when we're rich and famous we'll stay in places like this,' Toby said with mock-romance.

I laughed. But despite our playing, I felt something serious and promising here. OCD had obliterated my sense of The Future a long time ago, and now, on this holiday, I'd been surprised by a feeling of looking beyond, by a hint of the blissful clarity I might enjoy if I could stop my obsessive doubts and keep my feelings unambiguous. I needed to bottle this moment, but how?

Grand gestures are tricky to make when you're an obsessive. When you've got something to ask someone, something *important*, there's always the risk that something heinously inappropriate will come wobbling into your mind and squat all over the moment. But I felt like I had to give it a shot anyway.

Tomorrow would be awards night in London. The city's production companies would be quaffing coke and champagne into the wee hours in celebration of our most talented filmmakers. And Toby was here with me instead of there with them. Since he'd arrived I'd told him a thousand times how much that meant to me, and each time he'd held my face or put me on his lap and said that there was no dilemma – that there was nowhere he'd rather be. But I *so* wanted to make him feel special and make *us* feel special. Make this holiday feel special. I wanted more, more, more of our good feelings.

Brits Abroad

Jacks was a beautiful bamboo restaurant built onto the side of an old Portuguese-style family home. A palm tree trunk in the middle shouldered the sagging tarp roof and red fairy lights twisted around its bark. Catholic idols adorned the mint green walls and behind the bar there was a plastic mirror bearing the face of the Virgin Mary. Pink LED lights flashed around the aged glass. Jacks was run by a couple in their late middle age, and their speechless teenage son who took the orders. A couple of giddy younger boys flitted around, chasing the occasional stray cat under the bamboo chairs. There was never anyone else in there but us, and it'd become a sort of local.

Today, after a lazy lunch there, Toby had gone to the nearby internet café around the corner, which gave me the chance to set the wheels of my surprise in motion. I asked the old lady with a mixture of words and hand gestures if we could come back tonight. She nodded and smiled.

I then asked her if they had any champagne, miming the shaking and uncorking of a bottle. Following the enthusiastic beating of my hands she smiled and nodded the way you do when you're pretending to have heard something someone's said in a nightclub. Seeing she hadn't understood, I pointed to champagne on the menu, and she shook her head gravely.

'No, no, no, champen no,' she said, then sighed regretfully before shuffling off into her mint green house.

I wasn't sure if that was the end of the exchange, and wavered in the doorway until she hurried – almost skipped – back a minute later, with her peach sari clasped in one hand.

'Champen orkey,' she said, beaming.

'Brilliant, thank you so much.'

I should have left it there. With my non-existent Konkani and her patchy English, we'd been lucky to get this far. But I wanted a little extra flourish for Toby, so I handed her a note.

'Could you possibly bring this out with the bottle at dinner, please?' She ran it through her fingers, cooing girl-ishly, then pressed it to her chest.

Fearing that she'd got the wrong end of the stick, I motioned with more laboured hand-wanking that she please put it with the champagne. And she nodded with excitement and said 'yes, yes, yes', looking at me with grandmotherly pride before darting off back into the house, clutching the note between two palms.

I stood alone in the middle of the bar for a few moments, which was completely still save for the flies and the fan. I'd been introduced to Goans' phenomenal capacity for impro-visation a couple of days earlier when I'd ordered a potato salad at a restaurant, and the chef had substituted cherry tomatoes with glacé cherries.

This might be interesting, I thought.

When we got to Jacks that night the old couple were stood behind the bar in fancy outfits, smiling from ear to ear. The little boys were up and dressed smartly, too, and stood looking at us, giggling.

Definitely going to be interesting.

We sat down at 'our' table and ordered. Toby sat with his back to the bar, and over his shoulder I could see the family's eyes on me, waiting for 'the big signal'. I couldn't bear to look.

After placing our drinks on the table I saw the silent older son shrug at his parents. Then there was a lot of whispering and I saw the old man prod the old woman, who came over to our table tapping her fingers together in front of her chest.

'Madam, you want bortel?'

'Yes please.'

She nodded at the two small boys behind the bar, who whinnied and jumped up and down, and I burst out laughing. Toby took my hand and furrowed his brow.

'What are you laughing at?' he said.

'Nothing,' I said. The old couple were bickering about something they were preparing behind the bar.

'What are you laughing at? What did she say?' He took his hand away and folded his arms.

'Nothing – I don't know.'

'No.' He pulled it back. 'Tell me what you're laughing at.'

'Okay,' I sighed, 'so I came in earlier to order a bottle of champagne to toast your nomination–'

' – Arrrr. Yes! Treats. Thanks, lover.'

' – And I don't know what they think the occasion is but they're making quite a big thing of it and—oh no–'

' – What?' Behind Toby's shoulder I could see the old

couple ceremoniously approaching with all three sons following them in formal procession.

'Nothing. It's fine, just don't get embarrassed. I'm sorry.' Toby turned to discover that he'd been thrust into the centre of a full on *moment:* the shining, solemn faces all around him and the bottle being offered to him – appropriately enough – like a trophy. Baffled, touched, we both smiled widely at them and thanked them profusely, then there was an awkward five or so seconds when they lingered by the table, as though they were expecting something else to happen, before ambling back to the bar and watching us to see what would unfold.

Flushed pink by now, I placed both my palms on the sides of my face.

'Oh no.'

'What?'

'There was supposed to be a note.'

'What did it say?'

'Nothing.'

'Lover?'

'Just, "Thank you, I love you." I don't know where it is now. Maybe she thought it was for her.'

'Thank you for what?'

'For being here.'

'Love, I told you—'

'—but I know how much the awards mean to you,' I said, leaning towards him, 'so I booked us one night at the Intercontinental—'

'Okay, don't look at the lampshade.' I looked at the lampshade where a four-inch long locust was sat, almost touching my head, and I screamed.

Horrified that his only guests should be distressed, the old man came gallantly flapping with a tea towel, and mine and Toby's giggle fits started over again. As our host crunched the locust's meaty body under his shoe, I reached for my glass, arms shaking through suppressed laughter, and put it to my lips. Mid swig, I saw the old man cast me a quizzical glance.

'Are you just going to drink it like that, then?' Toby said with mock-horror.

I looked down to see the champagne bottle in my two hands. Toby was laughing so hard he could only speak to say 'Brits abroad' before burying his face in his menu.

'No– we can't–', I said, barely breathing and shaking my head, 'they'll think we're laughing at them.'

'Oh don't,' Toby said, pressing his palm to his chest and biting his bottom lip, 'that's a heartbreaker.' And suddenly, looking about us at the dead locust and the empty restaurant and the family's kind, puzzled faces behind the bar, we didn't know whether to laugh or cry.

Trying to regain composure Toby picked up the dessert menu. 'I reckon I could squeeze in a little one.'

'Could you squeeze in a *dessert,* as well?'

'After your champagne-necking they probably wouldn't even be surprised . . .' he said, taking an invisible pudding from an imaginary waiter's hands and squeezing it into his arse. 'All bought and paid for mate. Deal with it.'

Later, after a cuddly goodbye with the old couple, we snaked along the hot road home, giggling. Toby pulled me to him by the waist.

'I'm so glad it was weird, Lennie, I wouldn't have had it

any other way,' he whispered into my ear. 'And thank you for booking us into the hotel. It's gonna be wazzy isn't it?'

Tomorrow we'd be staying in the most overtly romantic place I'd ever seen, and as we fumbled giddily with the key in the lock, Piggle scuttling in the dark, wanting to join the party, I tried to forget that I'd already pictured the half-naked bodies which were waiting for me beside the Inter-continental's postcard perfect pool.

Purple Rain

I never believed in 'the one' in a cosmic sense. I'd always thought it was kind of bigheaded to assume that there was someone else on the earth whom fate had marked out for you, someone whose purpose it is to fulfil your mutual destiny and be your soulmate, to *complete* you. But I did believe in earth-shaking, all-consuming love, and ever since I was a little girl, imagining Christmas trysts with Macaulay Culkin – we'd foil the plots of baddies together and roam a snowy New York – I knew that I wanted that love with a boy. Now my OCD had melted that dream.

Since the quasiboyf at uni I'd recoiled from romance repeatedly, using each man's minor shortcomings to justify my callousness. When they'd tried to prise apart my clenched fists I'd winced and avoided eye contact, and curved my spine away from attempts at tenderness.

All through my New Rose therapy I'd remained free-spirited and happy-go-lucky on the surface. My friends would lean in around pub tables wearing 'tell us more' faces, sliding pints away from the edges, to hear how I'd been swept off my feet or landed myself in some romantic farce. And I'd lap up their disbelieving shrieks greedily, even though I was telling them about a vicarious life I felt I hadn't lived. Because no matter how ostensibly perfect my dates had been – Miami highrise or Thai waterfront – the OCD had taken me far, far away from those moments and those men.

'You're repellent,' said the last man who'd felt anything for me. 'I actually feel you repel me when I touch you.' And I did. When he swaggered into my life and wooed me with prepaid taxis and too-expensive dinners, I fought like a dog getting its claws clipped. I repelled him when he played Linkin Park on the guitar too earnestly. I repelled him when he detailed his gym routine. I repelled him when he tried to read me his poetry. His generosity, his sentimentality, his arrogance, his unabashed romance, the fact that he liked me and told me so often, his desire to share my problems. I abhorred it all. 'They're not your problems, they're our problems,' he'd say. I balked. My problems were *my* problems, insurmountably, and his efforts to shoulder them only reminded me that their weight was mine alone. 'Your heart's not open, Rose,' he said to me on the last day I saw him. Even the unrestrained poeticism of that parting phrase made me squirm.

So, of all the things I expected to be leaving behind when I got on board the bus for the round-the-world trip, a relationship wasn't one of them. But when I met Toby, six months before I was due to go, I very quickly loved him.

On our first date we drank and talked until morning, laughing into our pints and getting beer foam in our eyebrows, exchanging childhood anecdotes. How his family dogs are buried in the back garden wearing clip-on earrings. How one Christmas our dog blasted diarrhoea all over Pat's pile of freshly-opened presents, leaving not a single gift unscathed. How, during Maggie's boyfriend's first dinner at our family home, my Dad had bowled into the kitchen demanding to know who'd been 'spitting on the woodlice in the back loo'. No need for airs and graces here. In each other we saw the priceless life-fire that you get from having worn shit trainers at school.

The OCD was there, of course, it was never not there: intrusive doubts about whether a heterosexual romance was contrary to my inner desires. But there was something so specifically wonderful about this budding relationship that made me hopeful in a way that I'd never been before.

The first few months were fantastically impractical and inert, spent in our tiny Hackney bedrooms watching *Curb* and *Planet Earth* and eating giant beige dinners of pasta and butter, or out on missions for biscuits. We'd turn Lidl trips into protracted, stomach-aching affairs, stymied by the ribald inspection of dubious vegetables and bum-slaps in empty aisles.

I was falling more and more in love every day, and, in correlation, every day my OCD was getting worse, buckling under the weight of what I newly stood to lose if my obsessive doubts were true. Every day was a tussle between aching sadness and aching happiness and I didn't know which would win.

Toby understood what it was to chain smoke at a party out of nerves, and what it was to be acutely self-conscious. He let me be absent from him, vacant in his presence without asking, 'What are you thinking?' One night we were stood on his balcony looking over the roofs towards Bethnal Green, listening to 'Ignition' booming from the warehouse across the street, when he talked to me, unprompted, about the disparity between what a person was supposed to be feeling at any given moment, and what a person was actually feeling. I toked on my fag, watching him watching the sky, the supposed-tos and shoulds of all my life going up in smoke. It didn't matter about everyone else, everywhere, because in obsession-free slivers of time like these, I had someone with me on this side of the glass.

One evening about three months into our relationship, I met him on Regent's Canal after work and we walked towards Victoria Park Village to grab a Vietnamese. I was anxious and exhausted from a day of constant Os and Cs, and I could barely look at him. I'd struggled that day in particular because I'd had to give a group tutorial about editorial house style and one of my tutees had been wearing a low cut top, so that while delineating the finer points of that website's nauseatingly 'quirky' tone of voice, I'd been blinking through a great tumble of tits.

What did he think was going on in these moments when I so inexplicably withdrew from him? I still hadn't told him about my obsessions. How could I? 'I love you and P.S. I might be gay'? No, I couldn't. I wanted to, but I couldn't. I couldn't tell anyone for that matter. Who would believe me? If it was the other way around and someone told *me* that they were having unwanted thoughts about being gay, I'd probably assume they were struggling to come out, and that their attempts to medicalise their experience amounted to suppression – a potentially harmful grapple with the truth. It's another of OCD's tightly bound knots: because most people don't know that the disorder can encompass themes like sexuality, paedophilia and violence, obsessives stay silent for fear of others' incredulity – an incredulity they even feel themselves. *What if it really is just bullshit?* they think. So, through deep-rooted shame and self-censorship, ignorance breeds ignorance.

When Toby and I sat down at the Vietnamese, he held up his phone to my face and showed me a pixellated screen shot:

Prince. Stade de France, Paris. 30 juin 2011. Deux billets achetés.

'You bought them?', I asked, mouth open. A few days' before I'd sent him an impulsive text saying I'd seen an advert for a Prince gig in Paris, and that I'd gotten excited at the thought of us going. I'd tempered my thinly veiled infatuation by saying it was probably a daft, impractical idea.

He nodded.

I bit my lip and yelped and leant over the table to kiss him, knocking over his full pint glass and setting fire to my hair on the candle in the middle of the table, which sent smoke billowing above my head and the waitresses flapping. I hardly sat on my seat for the rest of the meal, squeezing his knees under the tablecloth and picking singed hair from my lap. He watched circumspectly with a raised eyebrow of mock disapproval as my food remained virtually untouched on my plate, which redoubled my giddiness.

The following month lilted with puppyness. Lying in bed or sitting on a bus or waiting in a queue, I'd get close to his ear and say,

'Guess what?'

'What?'

'We're going to see Prince in Paris!'

Often, late at night, impassioned, kazoo-style renditions of 'Purple Rain' would be hummed into armpits, or 'Kiss' percussion drummed on a pinned chest. Much belly fat was pinched in excitement. And I *was* excited, genuinely. But I was also afraid. I was afraid that this perfect gig with this beautiful man would pass me by. I was afraid that the dancers would be wearing tiny outfits, and that when Toby kissed me, their crotches would flash up between our lips and take me far away from him. It all felt so perverse in the face of this new love.

The shoulds and supposed-tos were creeping back.

At the London Eurostar terminal on our way to Paris, Toby ate a mountain of nachos, having ordered large in the expectation I'd be picking at them, as I usually did when I'd assured him I didn't want my own portion. But I genuinely wasn't hungry – it might have been the nerves – so he had that trough of guacamole all to himself, and it'd induced a comically irrepressible case of diarrhoea by the time we crowned on the continent. After waiting half an hour for him to emerge from the Gare du Nord toilets, I assured him we'd arrive discreetly at my aunt's apartment and relax.

Not so. Cue formal spread of three course meal, family catch-ups in a foreign language and 'What do you do, Toby?' conversations. There was even one of my aunt's family friends there. ('Pile 'em all in,' Toby said later when we giggled about it, 'room for one more'). Seeing him very graciously flash watery smiles in all the right places made me want to put him to bed and get all nurse-y on him, which I promptly did, because when the board of viscous cheese was presented, he broke out in a nervous sweat.

I lead him from the table, explaining his predicament to the French. 'Wine' was the unanimous advice, thoroughly sincere, 'he needs wine'.

The next day we entered the mouth of the Metro at Place de Clichy and I got anxious in the crowds and hid my face in Toby's neck. He'd intuited that when I rested my head against him like that, I needed protecting from something inside me, and his default mode in times like these was making me laugh, so he'd squeeze my bum to the rhythm of whichever tune we'd been humming that day, or snuffle the top of my head like a dog.

Inside the Stade de France we edged close to the stage, beers in hand, and stopped about ten metres back. It was still light when the crowd exploded to the sight of Prince, stage left. There he was, my hero, sleazing out his first vocal and stomping to bar after bar of unapologetic, progressive funk. Here I was, trying to imagine how I'd feel if the women in the band de-robed mid-song in an Bucks-fizz-at-Eurovision flourish; imagining it in great detail, *anticipating* it, as if it was actually about to happen, crossing my fingers for briefs instead of G-strings.

The OCD thoughts had amassed in such high numbers that the simple pleasure of music was now being trampled under a bigger, louder parade. It was drowning out the things I loved.

'Can I come over there?' Prince asked the right side of the crowd coquettishly, making them scream. 'But . . . but,' he wavered with a smirk of faux indecision, 'can I come over *there*?' he asked the left side. Then he slapped out a bass solo and the whole stadium swooned as one, and I was back on the other side of the glass with my OCD and the press of bodies all around me.

Am I enjoying the brush of that woman's arm?
Should Prince be turning me on?
Would French knickers be okay?

The band hulked out hit after hit for 90 minutes, well beyond the sunset, so that when the blackout came it was truly black. The crowd was electric as it waited for the encore. Then the lights came back up – purple – and the famous piano started looping over and over and Prince's voice came in rich and strong, 'I never meant to cause you any trouble, I never meant to cause you any pain'. I felt Toby's hands around my waist and he lifted me so that my feet rested on two upturned beer glasses which he'd arranged on the floor like bucket stilts, and I turned around and watched 50,000 white lights waving softly in the dark. The guitar solo cued a sparkling rush of ticker tape into the air, and millions of purple and gold slivers floated to the ground, snapping into sight when they caught the light, like fish in sunlit water. I leant my back against Toby's chest before turning round to kiss him when the song finished, and for a tiny, precious moment, I was there, feeling my heart shimmering in my chest. Feeling what Love was supposed to be.

Tell Suckah

Like most 14-year-olds, I usually came home from school and slumped on the sofa, exhausted with hormones, and played the Megadrive until *Neighbours*. The problem with *Neighbours* was you had to endure the double torture of *Newsround* and *Blue Peter* before entering into the kingdom of Ramsay Street. But it was worth the suffering.

The dog knew that the two-minute sliver between *Neighbours* and *The Simpsons* meant that me and Patty would kick off, big time, usually with quarrels about who was going to fetch the remote from the sideboard. Such disputes were often settled with a swift game of Muscle In, whereby you'd lie full length on the sofa, rigid and immovable, while the other tried to muscle you off the edge. It took the dog a couple of years' conditioning, but eventually she associated the *Neighbours* theme tune with trouble, so that whenever she heard it she'd come barging into the lounge, barking. And even if we were sitting quietly, she'd mistrust our calm

My OCD had not yet begun, and so I could, and did, watch the telly for hours and hours, unencumbered. *Gladiators* had finished that year, and though this had been a seemingly irreparable injury at the time, I'm now glad that it finished before my OCD could claim it. Fashanu and Jonsson would only have ending up having fok on the crash mats.Wolf and Hunter, too. Who knows what Hang Tough would've looked like.

But one afterschool session was uncommonly TV-free.

As I turned the front door handle I felt strange vibrations pulsing through the brass into my palm. I entered cautiously and paused in the middle of the hall, trying to figure out the deep, deep sounds which were coming from Ted's bedroom. Mom's trinkets rattled on the shelf below the mirror and I looked at my reflection in the quivering glass. My hair was ravaged by repeated gonzo Sun-In applications: nothing new there, but my lips were doing something I hadn't seen them do before – a kind of pouty frown. The dog looked at me suspiciously as my battered Head backpack slid off my shoulders and my outsized adolescent feet began to tap out a rhythm on the carpet.

'What is it?', I whispered to the hound, mind blown. It was the first time I'd ever heard funk.

The same day I borrowed all of Ted's CDs and cassettes and fell in love. Cameo and Parliament and Bootsy Collins. The sound was massive and so was the artwork: neon pinks and lime greens and cosmic starscapes; men in heels and waist-high glittery leggings and oversized intergalactic, spangled sunglasses; and amazing, buff women with giant afros. In my grey-and-navy school uniform I listened and listened and listened, and went with them to New York and Detroit and to worlds I'd never dreamed of.

As the months passed I saved up the money I made working on the till at a garden centre to buy a bass guitar. It was way too big and heavy for my body and I could barely play it, but it was the most precious thing I'd ever owned and I loved it so much.

One day I managed to pinpoint the song I'd heard coming through Ted's wall that first afternoon: 'One Nation Under a Groove' by Funkadelic. The lyrics aren't about love or about boys and girls, they're a tribute to the hugeness of the sound:

> So wide you can't get around it.
> So low you can't get under it.
> So high you can't get over it.
> This is a chance
> To dance your way
> Out of your constrictions
> Tell suckah.

'Yes. Yes. YES,' I said when I read them, sat crossed legged on my bedroom floor, munching a Toffee Crisp. 'So wide you can't get around it'. That's *exactly* what it felt like. The sound was so wide and so mighty that it could overpower my niggling adolescent worries, and when I got older, it could sometimes even overpower my OCD. It was like there was only room for *one* parade in my brain, and the funk was the loudest – a supercharge current buzzing all along my neurons, in a dazzle of sequins and platforms, filling the pathways in my brain with its rainbow light, causing all other mental noise to briefly kneel and let it pass, if only for a few, fleeting moments.

Black Country Nails

But fleeting moments were not enough. Happiness was losing and depression set in.

One morning about a month after the Prince gig, I woke up crying so hard that Toby had to dress me like a child, pulling socks over my limp feet and a T-shirt over my bowed head. He was wont to chitchat at moments like these to try and rally me round, and as he lifted my chin from my chest he said something about how surprisingly heavy the human head is. I remember thinking with a blackness characteristic of real, distortive, masochistic, self-pitying depression, that my head was heavier than anyone could ever possibly know.

As he pulled my T-shirt down over my chest he saw the superficial cuts on my ribcage, which unlike the old ones on my arm were fresh and had recently bled. He sat on the floor and put his head in his hands and for the first time he sobbed.

'I don't know what's going on, Rose, and I don't know what I can do to help.'

'Neither do I.'

'I don't know what to do. I don't know what to do.'

'Neither do I.'

'What did you *use*?' he said, scanning the room. On the

shelf behind him lay a fishing knife. 'How can you do that to yourself?'

'I'm so sorry.'

That night I lay in bed alone thinking about what was I doing to him with my secret condition. It was five weeks before I was due to travel the world in a bus full of strangers. I needed help. I needed love. I needed to tell the truth.

So the following morning I caught a train back to the Midlands. I didn't know how the hell you were supposed to tell your parents that your mind is plagued with hardcore sexual thoughts. But for my life's sake I had to try.

I lingered in the alleyway from the train station where I'd lingered many times. Once, when he was a kid, Patty had got shot with a BB gun here, prompting Dad and Ted to tear down the road, fists in the air, shouting at the sky. I liked that when it came to family, the men in my life were as hard as Black Country nails.

I came out of the alley onto the street, but walked the long way round through the moss-smelling copse and the dark wet park, putting off going home. The damp, peaty funk of memories filled my head as I sat beneath the dripping lime trees on the same wall I'd sat on ten years before, when I'd seen that first thunderbolt image of a naked little boy. Rationally I now know that it'd been a product of mental disorder, and that my current identity doubts were, too. But rationality had changed nothing. As I watched the distant streetlight coming through the trees as it always used to, I was struck by the great gyres of time that mental illness consumes – not day by day but life by life – flouting so spectacularly the stories we're told about Closure and Time Heals.

The street had always been the same – the same Duplo drain covers, the same curby curbs, the same tarmac lines I used to tread with meticulous care. Some of the neighbours had laid paves on their driveways and some had double glazed their windows or put bronze knockers on their doors, but apart from the steady accumulation of these suburban prizes, there was a changelessness here which unsettled me. Places which should have been reminiscent of first kisses and drunken giggles now aroused in me an intangible fear – a ghost image of a thousand long-forgotten obsessions, burnt almost imperceptibly into the eye of my mind.

Wandering up the street I considered turning around and getting a train back to London. There would still be connections to Birmingham at this time. I stopped a few houses short, wavering. *Should I even be telling them?* As kids we put all of our childish might into trying to protect our parents, like the tiny owlet who puffs out its feathers in a show of strength that isn't there. Telling them would counter that most natural urge. But I had to do it.

When Toby'd calmed down after seeing the cuts, he'd apologised and assured me that everything was fine. But I knew our relationship would undoubtedly end if my condition carried on as it was. Despite my vow never to do so, I would surely overpower him with my weakness.

I reached the threshold and rested my head on the textured glass of the porch. I turned the handle – the door was unlocked as always – and stepped with a deep breath onto the carpet in the hall, still threadbare where the dog used to scratch it. I reckon if you looked hard enough you could still find tufts of white fur pinched in the loose joints of the wooden chairs, their rungs pulped by a teething puppy long ago. The dog had known all my secrets.

Round the living room door I saw my mom's silver head, and the tip of the crossword. Dad sat next to her watching the TV with the volume down low, hovering his finger over the remote in a perpetual state of readiness, as always, as though the TV might try to out-fox him at any moment and spontaneously change channels.

I listened for a minute. It was a programme about the Brontës that Dad had undoubtedly seen fifty times already. While Dad's taste in literature was wildly sentimental, Mom had little patience for the Romantics, and they were constantly ribbing each other about it. Now, over her crossword, Mom periodically groaned at the hammy voiceover.

'Listen to the *passion*, cherie,' Dad said, raising his hand into a thespian claw. 'Heathcliff. HEATHCLIFF.' He squeezed Mom's knee and she squealed.

'Mom?' I said, guiltily, holding out my arms.

Seeing my face she stood up, shocked but not showing it, and put her arms around me. '*Qu'est-ce qu'il y a, bébé?*'

'Dear Rose,' Dad said, stroking my hair.

I slumped between them on the sofa and rested my head on his chest, where as a child I'd loved to listen to his big heart boom-booming, like the steps of a big bear far away. It meant safety then, and it did now. They waited for me to finish crying before they asked me anything.

'What's the matter, *ma biche?*'

This is it, I thought. *My chance to take off the mask.* I looked down at their wrinkling hands, which'd always held mine like this when I'd needed them. I opened my mouth but

I had nothing to say so I closed it again. *I can't. I just can't. I just can't.* It was too preposterous. Too pathetic. Who'd believe me? How was I going to word it? 'I'm not gay but I think about it all the time and I can't enjoy my relationship because I keep having graphic sexual thoughts about women?' *It's bullshit, how can I say it?* I couldn't. I had to stay quiet. I had to censor myself.

In the past I'd told them generic things about my 'repetitive thoughts', but I'd never gone into detail or told them how bad it was or invited them to ask questions, and I'd used words like anxiety and depression: general terms that were easy to understand and not technically fibs. *I won't tell them the truth, but I won't lie either,* I thought, as I took a deep breath.

'I just get so many intrusive thoughts in my head all the time and I can't do anything about them. I've been feeling so depressed lately.'

'Oh, Rosey,' Dad said, kissing the top of my head.

Mom smiled an encouraging smile and squeezed my hand tighter. 'It's okay, *bibiche*, we're here.'

The following day Dad had knocked on my bedroom door tentatively – the profusion of poorly concealed erotica books in my room had taught my parents long ago to enter with caution.

'Hello, Rose,' he said, standing apologetically in the middle of the room, 'Me and Mom have been talking,' he gestured through the wall where I knew Mom would be trying to busy herself folding clothes or doing the crossword, 'and we want to say that we'll make the right therapy happen, whatever it takes. You don't need to worry about it.'

I looked at my lap, embarrassed by the sudden tears in my eyes. I knew they couldn't afford it. Dad looked old standing there in top-to-toe Marks & Spencer and his Lidl trainers that he'd been so proud of when he'd found them in the bargain basket – lime green high tops which he wore without laces as slippers around the house – the kind of 'give-a-fuck?' flourish which'd mortified me when I was a teenager, but which I now so deeply appreciated. At school I'd thought the other kids' dads were cool in their Adidas fleeces and Caterpillar boots. Little did I know that *my* dad was killing it all along.

'Thank you,' I said.

He nodded his grey head and said 'Okay then' with a little smile, and kissed the air at me before leaving, padding softly across the carpet. But I knew that inside he was tearing down the road with his fists in the air for me.

Buttery Toast

I recuperated at my parents' house for a week, and was blindsided by their thousand tiny acts of tenderness: endless hot drinks and books and buttery toast. They were heroes.

'*Biche*,' Mom said, stroking my face, a few days into my visit, 'are you sure you're well enough to go on the trip?'

'I've got to, Mom, no doubt. It'll be fine, I promise. I'm going to find some therapy before I go. Then the time away will give me a chance to put into practice everything I've learned. Then when I come back the thoughts will be better and things with Toby will be better. It's got to happen this way, trust me.'

'Okay, *lapin*,' she said, worried. 'But *please* let me take you to France first.' She was already pleading. I guess she knew how stubborn I could be.

'Okay, *Maman*.'

She was hooked up with this awesome shrink in Paris, and a couple of days later I was sat in his surgery, holding Mom's hand.

'The doctor will see you now,' the receptionist said in French.

I walked to the consultation room door and looked back before entering. Mom was smiling and nodding little nods, just like she did when she took me the bedwetting clinic when I was five years old. I'd been glad she was with me then and I was glad she was with me now.

'*Bonjour mademoiselle,*' the doctor said.

'*Bonjour monsieur.*'

I told him in hesitant French that I had '*pensées intrusives*' – intrusive thoughts – but still could not bring myself to tell him the whole truth. He prescribed me paroxetine – another SSRI anti-depressant, commonly prescribed for OCD – assuring me it wouldn't turn me into a zombie like the other one I'd tried, and that it really would help lessen the intensity of the doubts. On reflection he was probably right, but by now I was mistrustful of drugs, and though I went through the motions of going to the pharmacy and picking them up, I knew I'd never take them.

Back at my folks' house I researched possible therapies long and hard online. Yes, I'd had bad experiences with shrinks in the past, but I knew so much more about OCD now, and I was so much better placed to make a sound decision.

I found this one place with a pro website and a wordy manifesto. They offered a five-day OCD therapy course, which was perfect, as I'd have time to do it before I left in five weeks' time. It was eye-wateringly expensive and would be bought with money that my parents didn't have. I couldn't mess it up. This therapy had to save me.

The course was a lot of money. £1000 reduced from £2000. This would be bought with money that my parents didn't have and I wouldn't be able to pay them back quickly. I couldn't mess it up.

When I phoned one of the UK's largest OCD charities to ask for a second opinion on the course, they warned me emphatically not to do it, explaining that I should be extremely wary of any therapist who strayed from a tried-and-tested regime of exposure therapy and cognitive behavioural therapy. Effectively calling the course leader a charlatan, the advisor said that he'd had countless complaints from dissatisfied clients, who'd felt ritually humiliated by some of the course's exercises. I put down the phone and sobbed. He had to be wrong. This *had* to be the course to make me better.

I ignored other warning signs, too. Having emailed the course leader asking whether or not all her staff were registered with the BABCP, she replied: 'I believe that all of my current therapists are accredited.' It was a non-committal response and it might have set alarms bells ringing had I not been so obsessively desperate for a resolution, had my compulsive fixation on a cure not impaired my judgment so completely.

Later, on the phone, when I told her what the OCD charity had advised, she accused them of slander, and assured me of her methods' efficacy. Indeed, she was so appalled that she offered to discount some of my course fee.

I'd already warmed to her. This person was going to be my saviour.

Shangri-La

From the hot shade of the parasol I could see the carved lawn curve down to the sea, the little colonial club huts with their stacks of crisp white towels outside, the pattering sprinklers spraying wet rainbows into the air and golfers resting in the shade of the beachside palms. Behind me I could see the vast colonial palace of yellow and white marble, the teak ceiling fans spinning in silent glossy circles in the verandah, the seafood barbecue on its paved terrace. I could smell the cumin'd paneer popping, rich and gloopy, and the prawns, their pink ridges curling against the steel, the lemon searing on their skin.

Across the pool's perfect water she arched her back, wife to the Russian millionaire who was squatting to take her photo, spreading his thighs to accommodate his ripe paunch. She basted herself with oil, knowingly lingering near her fake breasts as the shutter clicked. I knew that for the rest of the day, the rest of the week, month or year, my OCD would hold her aloft like a prize – triumphant over everything I was supposed to be feeling on this paradisiacal day.

Next to me my beautiful boyfriend lay, holding my hand.

Rising from the sun lounger he tried to pull me up.

'Are you coming in?' he said, pointing towards the pool and tugging at me playfully.

Raising my head to look at him, I saw the water glisten on

his chest, the sea-sun behind him catching the blond in his beard, the bewitching concoction of boyishness and masculinity.

'I think I'll stay here, baby. You go.' I tried to smile.

He bowed his head as he walked alone to the water's edge.

This was supposed to be the big send off, the big I love you, the big you-mean-more-to-me-than-anything. But the Russian and her fat millionaire had invaded it. They had fucked all over the Goa Intercontinental and they fucked all over the rest of our holiday, entering my mind once a minute for three consecutive days.

And however much I tried, I could not eradicate the possibility that I didn't have OCD after all. I could not chemically obliterate the doubt that seeing that woman naked in my mind, time and time again, meant that the future I so desperately wanted with Toby was a great, sad lie.

Two days of tears passed. Two days of Toby trying to cheer me with chitchat and little games: skimming stones or making lists of all the animals we'd seen, and I didn't smile once. Feeling like this on a rainy Tuesday in Hackney didn't matter much. No-one noticed. But here, among the palms and stars, in what's supposed to be a romantic Shangri-La, my failing was blatant. And I still couldn't tell him about the thoughts, because I was still clinging to a brittle ideal that'd shatter if I did.

Now it was the morning of Toby's leaving. At the breakfast table he sat opposite me at first, but soon moved to sit beside me and placed his hands on mine.

'Shhh,' he said, trying to stop me from shaking. We ordered omelettes and masala tea and ate quietly. As soon as he put his cutlery down I pulled his arm around me.

Under our table a wild dog sniffed for scraps before spiralling a couple of times and slumping down in the sand with a hmmphf. He was a welcome distraction, and we both leant forward to fuss him, tickling the top of his ears, and ruffling his nape. I lazily cupped a handful of sand into a little pile onto his back.

'Awww, don't be mean,' Toby said.

'Oh, but it's okay to cover its *asshole* with sand?'

Toby grinned, having forgotten about the night at Brendan's. 'He liked it.'

The taxi beeped outside and we said goodbye on the pavement. It'd be ten weeks before we saw each other again. Toby held my head and whispered again and again that it would be okay. He lifted my glasses from my face. I'd told him a couple of days before that every time he did so he scraped the glasses' nasal pads against my forehead and it hurt. And now he always did it with the concentrated care of a child who's been trusted to hold the class hamster. He looked into my eyes solidly and did this little nod of the head. And I nodded back without saying anything. He thumbed away some mascara flecks from my face, kissed me, and got into the waiting car.

'I'm going to make myself better,' I whispered, as the taxi snaked off up the road. 'I've said that before, but I mean it this time.'

100% Bad

'Do you want to go out on a date?' I asked the woman in the pencil skirt. She looked me up and down with a confused smile, shook her head and walked away. Another woman sashayed past in heels and I asked her the same question, shaking. The same answer came. She clopped up the paving stones and I watched the jiggle of her ass with every step.

Maybe I fancy her?

No.

I am having an OCD thought.

I am having an OCD thought.

I am having an OCD thought.

I was sat on a wall at the side of the road. I leant down and picked at the lichen on the bricks, sending citrine flakes quivering to the ground and chunks of green moss tumbling. I felt sick. I had to stay sitting for many minutes before I was able to get up and go.

I was performing a task at the behest of the therapist on my five-day therapy course. Today, he'd instructed me to stop three women in the street – strangers – and ask them if they wanted to go on a date. Other exercises included asking the Science Museum staff where the 'special section for gay people' was, asking people for directions to the nearest lesbian bar, staring a newsagent proudly in the eye while buying a lesbian porno mag over the counter, and rating Girls Aloud's tits out of ten.

It was group therapy. On the first day we'd all sat around a large oval table in the front room of a soulless Victorian terrace in darkest North London. The kind with those singularly depressing vertical window blinds with the cords that get all yellowed and tangled. No-one was looking at anyone. It was the first time I'd met anyone else with OCD. Not a moment of relief or solidarity, but alarm, to see what this condition looked like from the outside in: gaunt, shifty, suspicious.

The therapist had begun by showing us a short film about a Chilean earthquake. It showed families suffering unimaginable hardship: houses flattened, orphaned children wailing in the streets.

'If you think your life is shit, think again,' the therapist had said when the film ended. His point was indisputable: compared to large swathes of the human population, we were all staggeringly privileged, and our pain was nothing compared to that of these poor people. Here *I* was, about to embark on my *second* round-the-world trip. This was a wake-up call.

He'd gone on to explain that his course used a mixture of techniques to help his clients break down their irrational beliefs. 'Recovering from OCD is like recovering from addiction,' he'd said. 'It will take about six weeks for your brains to recover from your addiction to avoiding anxiety.'

'You did really well, Rose,' the therapist said when I got back from asking out the women. The exercise had been a form exposure and response prevention therapy (ERP), whereby an obsessive is repeatedly exposed to triggers until they habituate to the feared stimulus. As Pavlov's dogs were conditioned to salivate at the ring of a bell, the brain can be conditioned *not* to respond to a certain trigger.

There is a growing consensus among OCD experts that successful treatment of the condition must include some form of ERP. I knew this, and that's what had attracted me to this course in the first place – it seemed modern and on-point in a way that the Freudian 'sexual memory', 'inter-personal relationship' therapy had never done. What I'd done today was an extreme form of ERP called Flooding, whereby instead of *gradually* exposing obsessives and habit-uating them over time, starting with relatively tame triggers, they're plunged in at the deep end.

'I know that was hard for you,' the therapist said. I couldn't speak. He gave me a little squeeze on my upper arm. 'Take a tissue and sit yourself down, we'll give you a minute.'

The others were pale and jittering on the sofa, having just done exposures of their own, and I slumped down next to them. What I'd just experienced seemed brutal and counter-therapeutic (not that brutality and therapy are mutually exclusive: treatment for OCD absolutely *should* be chal-lenging. I once met a brilliant Maudsley Hospital therapist who made in-patients with paedophilia obsessions paint 'I'm a paedophile' in six-foot-high red letters all around their hospital rooms, wear 'I'm a paedophile' t-shirts around the grounds, and shout 'I'm a paedophile' from their windows). Years later I would ask a world-leading OCD specialist what he thought about Flooding, and he said that it can work very well, but that it was only ethical if the patient was fully aware of what was involved; otherwise the distress caused could be very damaging.

'How do you feel, Rose?'

'Absolutely horrendous—'

'Now, when you say "absolutely horrendous" you're awfulising, aren't you?' the therapist said. That morning he'd introduced us to the concept of 'awfulising', in reference to the human tendency to think that our problems couldn't get any worse. By using the 'non-awfulising' technique of listing the ways that things *could* be worse, he'd explained, we can learn to see our obsessions more rationally. 'Let's go back to the theoretical scenario from earlier. Do you really think it would be *100%* bad if you were, say, a paedophile?' he asked me.

'Yes. 100% bad,' It was unequivocal.

'Okay, can anyone suggest how Rose might challenge this irrational belief?'

No-one answered.

'Well, let's ask how it could be worse. Would it be worse, in theory, if you were not only a paedophile, but your family were dead?'

I nodded, grimly.

'Well, could we not say, then, that your original thought that "being a paedophile is 100% bad" is irrational, seeing as we've just hit on something that would make that situation a whole lot worse? You see, if we can remind ourselves that our feared situations wouldn't be so bad, we can lessen the impact of the obsessions.'

The last bit jarred with me, almost imperceptibly. The whole 'questioning of irrational beliefs' thing, which was at the heart of this course, was based on the assumption that there was something wrong with my beliefs about my obsessions – that there was some flawed philosophy unpinning it all. But somehow, though it wasn't yet a fully formed thought, I didn't think this was the case. After all, I categorically did *not* believe that it would be '100% bad' to be gay (on the contrary, I knew that if I was gay I'd just be *gay*, and it'd be cool, I'd have a right old time). My 'feared situation' was not *being gay* – it was never being able to know my sexuality for sure. Nor did I believe that experiencing involuntary mental images could say anything definitive about a person's sexuality. Nor did I believe that sexuality was black or white. I'd reached a point of my OCD where I'd gained a paradoxical insight: I knew, at a rational level, that all of my obsessions and compulsions were absurd, yet at a neurotic level I felt helplessly compelled to engage with them as though they were legitimate. If you're rationally aware of the irrationality of your mental processes, how can they be said to be governed by beliefs which need challenging?

But just as I'd trusted my psychodynamic therapist when she'd told me that my doubts were the product of sexual suppression, so I trusted this therapist when he told me that there was something wrong with my beliefs. I made myself quash my misgivings because I was about to travel the world on a job. And because I just *had* to get better.

'Now, apart from feeling horrendous, how did you get on charming the ladies of London?'

'I was so, so anxious every time I did it. Even though rationally I knew there was nothing to be scared of, my mind kept saying stuff like "you're only scared because you can't face the truth" and "this is what you really want."'

'And when your mind was saying those things, what did you do?'

'I said what you told me to say.'

'Great. Can you remind the group what that was?'

'"I am having an OCD thought."'

'Good work, Rose.'

'I don't know, though, it's so hard.' I looked out the window. 'I don't even care if I'm gay, I just keep thinking that I wouldn't feel like Me if I was, and if I'm not Me then what's even real?—'

'—I know, Rose, but listen, this is why we're learning what we're learning. If you carry on challenging your irrational beliefs, every day, soon you'll reach a point where you're more accepting of these possibilities.'

I nodded, but in my head I was storming at him because he'd said this a hundred times already today and was yet to wave his magic wand and make me better. I was giving him everything and in return I wanted him to be a god. In his mortality he was failing me. Then I got lost for half a minute imagining myself ranting across the table – *you have no idea, NO IDEA* – before realising that the sofa was shaking with the bobbing of my knee and that they were all looking at me.

If he was right, and I had to believe that he was, I'd be better in six weeks' time. And if my calculations were correct, that'd be just in time for my trip to the Taj Mahal.

Hentai

I started to hear a whirring sound – a rushing motion in my dreams, and I woke to the fan on full power fluttering the bedclothes around me. When I turned it off I could hear the crows on the windowsill, and the porn next door.

It sounded like Japanese hentai porn. The surface of the girl's eyes would be quivering, her large shiny breasts rising and falling with her snapped breaths; there'd be some forceful elfin boy putting his finger to her lips and some resistance from her – little yelps of pain and pleasure. I turned the fan back on and lay back down on the double bed – two singles pushed together, sweaty at the join.

I needed the bathroom, but right now I didn't fancy walking to the end of the corridor to the communal one, or handling the series of heavy padlocks which made your fingers smell of copper coins, or possibly bumping into Wanking Guy splashing his face at the basin—*or Wanking Girl . . . ? Was it a girl beating off in there?* A lump rose in my throat.

I'd arrived in Mumbai late last night after a short flight from Goa, and checked into the Salvation Army Hostel in Colaba. I'd hoped the stories of rats, mites and mould had been apocryphal, but they'd rang farcically true as soon as I'd stepped into my sweetsour-smelling room – a 12-foot-high pickle jar. The double doors were pale yellow and chipped, the walls salmon pink, all filthy and stained. Arched windows and dour furniture made it feel like a monastery cell, and it was musty like one, too. Films about paedo priests in 1950s Ireland are filmed in buildings like this. It was grimly fascinating.

I stared up at the fan and the little bits of chipped paint it was disturbing on the ceiling. In the corner of my eye I saw the blur of a cockroach darting across the bed.

'Fuck this.'

I leapt up and pulled on my denim shorts from the greasy floor tiles, sliding them over my bedbug-bitten thighs and hopping to the cast iron lattice window. I yanked open the curtains and the crows on the windowsill fireworked out into the sky until they were black specks against the blue. Another murder mobbed a buzzard in the distance. In the courtyard below, a man was sweeping with a twig broom.

Across the street an old mansion house, built by the British a hundred years ago, was rotting in the sunlight. Once white, it stood filthy and grey and massive, and the old paves around its base were broken up by an Indian willow tree, which tumbled thousands of vines from its great height to the floor below. They silhouetted and swayed in the light coming across the harbour.

I'd spent six days alone in Goa after Toby left, waiting for a date for the recommencement of the trip. I'd gone to the beach every day. Taken the scooter out into the mountains. Watched the monkeys. It was an idyllic kind of solitude – romantic really. Or at least it would have been if I hadn't been so busy.

Each day I'd lain on my bed for hours, thinking about how, exactly, I'd felt when I'd been with Toby; about how, exactly, I'd felt about the Michelangelo's David's penis guy at Oktoberfest; about how, exactly, I'd felt about the Russian wife in Goa. My daydreams about Toby became exercises in discernment: had I really been happy? It'd felt that way at the time. But had I been *perfectly* happy?

From that week's ruminations I'd made a concrete decision about my future, and from now on I was going to change tactics in making myself better. That first lovely day in Goa, in the hut with the muslin and palm shadows, I'd glimpsed what unthinkingness could feel like, and now I was going to make it mine, by force.

I was going to spend the rest of the trip stamping out my doubts like tropical roaches – hard to kill, yes, but not too hard. It was now clear that the 'I'm having an OCD thought' response was not working, but I had one weapon left in my arsenal: loop tapes. The intensive therapist had encouraged us to record ourselves repeating rational facts that we could listen to on loop every day.

I found one of my recordings on my laptop and hit 'play'. 'The following statements,' my shattered voice says, 'are all 100% true:

If I was sexually attracted to both men and women I could still enjoy my relationship with a man.

I can still enjoy my relationship if I'm aroused by women.

Many women in heterosexual relationships say they find women attractive.

Women's magazines are proof that heterosexual women enjoy looking at other women's bodies.

I don't have to be aroused by most men to be straight.

There is no law which states that heterosexual people must be aroused by the majority of the opposite sex.'

And so it went on, for over an hour.

When the therapist had first suggested the exercise I'd been sceptical. Something about it felt futile: of course I already knew that *rationally* these statements made sense, but in the split-second moment of obsession, a million hours' rationalisation never made a jot of difference. I guess somehow I'd intuited what I would later find out for sure: that in constantly reminding the obsessive-compulsive brain what's objectively true, we only feed its vicious cycle.

But I was running out of options and my desperation railroaded my better judgment. And that morning in that roach-infested room I made a fresh commitment to listen to these loop tapes at every opportunity. If I tried harder than I ever had, I could drive the doubts from my mind with reason.

This would be an extermination.

When the cartoon woman next door stopped coming, I went down for breakfast in the common room and sat under an amateur painting of Mother Theresa, whose bared teeth and tight lips were singularly ghastly – more cadaverous than canonic. It broke my heart a bit to think about its creator stepping from the canvas with a proud smile after the last, cack-handed brushstroke. I ate my breakfast of hard-boiled eggs, bread and fruit, trying not to make eye contact with the folks chowing bananas all around me, and listened to the loops through my headphones until the mass suck-off subsided.

After breakfast I left the hostel, on my way to meet the rest of the crew at a bar on the main strip, and stepped for the first time into an Indian city, listening to my loop tape through my headphones.

In the quavering heat I ogled the near-impossible dwellings – tiny rooms piled in corrugated iron on top of decrepit market stalls and shop fronts. Glimpses of men plying trades in cubby holes in their rafters. Launderettes and tobacco shops and travel agencies. Whole families lying together on dusty curbs amid paan splats and stray puppies. The beautiful little girls slipping tiny jasmine flower garlands around tourists' wrists. The scaly chickens. The paper box lanterns – orange, red and yellow – strung from building to building. And strung among them: Mother T and the hentai girl, gyrating.

'I can still enjoy my relationship if I'm aroused by women,' my voice said in my ears.

I got to the doorway of the bar and the crew waved me over, smiling. Erik patted the chair next to him so I took out my earphones and sat down. Hands came from all over the table to touch my cheek or my shoulders. Then came the how-are-yous and the tan comparisons, and my public persona reanimated quickly. I 'no-wayed?' and 'shut-upped?' through anecdotes about tales of whirlwind romances and beach sex and jungle raves, while under the table my thumbs were bleeding.

We left Mumbai in a flurry of excitement, naturally. Erik had plotted out an incredible adventure north via Udaipur,

Jaipur, New Delhi and Kathmandu, and my distress in the face of this experience felt increasingly incongruous.

We'd then be flying to Western Australia for the last leg of our journey: a two week drive from Perth to Sydney. Already there were whisperings among the crew of a beach festival in Perth, which was happening just two weeks before I planned to fly back to London and to Toby. Its expanse of half naked Australians would naturally be a savage gauntlet for my obsessions, so it seemed like a healthy milestone on which to set my sights. I absolutely *had* to be better by then.

But for now I was anticipating a more modest and more imminent challenge: Agra, Uttar Pradesh, where we'd join the three million annual visitors to the Taj Mahal. That big hunk of white stone would be a preliminary testing ground. If I could savour one of the seven wonders of the world without once thinking about sex, I'd know that the loop tapes were working.

If You Are Bad. I Am Your Dad . . . !

Agra, Uttar Pradesh, India. It was the morning of Taj Mahal day.

We girls had made ourselves up especially, knowing the photos taken over the next few hours would be ripe for Facebook. We'd already seen those photos in our minds – the sky a rich blue behind the eggshell mausoleum, its reflection perfect in the cerulean pool, us sat crossed legged on the marble bench, serene, framed by the minarets and the avenues of trees. If ever there was a day for make-up, this was it.

You're not allowed to drive a motorized vehicle within half a mile of the Taj Mahal because the pollution discolours its white stone. So the salesmen come on bicycles, selling snow domes and portable chess boards. We came by rickshaw before sunrise, weaving through the frenzied streets of Agra, past the slums and squatter settlements where half of the city's population now live. When we stopped in traffic child hawkers rushed through the fray of wheels with bags of nuts and marigold garlands. I checked my mascara in my hand mirror.

When we arrived at the grounds of the Taj, the queue for the box office outside the big arched doors flexed with tension. Tourists compulsively checked the sky for signs of the sun. This was not the postcard weather they'd been hoping for – if the clouds didn't clear those much anticipated trophy photos would be subpar. Is subpar really what you want to say about your holiday of a lifetime?

The clouds remained so that sunrise was merely an unremarkable fade from dark grey to light grey, and the fog sat heavy and low, so that the Taj Mahal was barely visible when we got to the top of the famous avenue. The reflecting pool reflected nothing. I watched as faces puckered behind camera screens – those few thousand pixels were disappointing.

I stood at the top of the marble steps and stared hard, squinting, waiting for a sense of the sublime to wash over me, some in-your-bones feeling of connectivity to the unfathomable history and humanity of this place. But, instead: deflation, and the strange uneasiness of my failed, plastic emotions; an imperfect enjoyment confounded by too much anticipation and too much mascara.

As we wandered down towards the mausoleum, stopping now and then to pose for jazz-hands photos and do-something-funny photos, I started to notice the couples taking it in turns to snog on the bench made famous by Princess Diana, who herself had presented a postcard version of her life to an expectant public. I saw myself sitting in their midst, on the marble between them, kissing and more. Discreetly, I put in one headphone and listened to the loop tape as we picked our way though the pristine manicured gardens towards the mausoleum. Under the epic dome's vaulted archways, I checked each tourist and tried to figure out how I'd feel kissing them, and before long I was buried in rumination, and the Taj Mahal's three million annual visitors were right here before me, arses aloft, presenting for inspection.

On the Taj Mahal's north side flows the huge Yamuna river, named after the goddess Yamuna, daughter of Sun and sister of Death. It has come from a Himalayan glacier 6000 metres high, twisting through forests of acacia and rosewood, bearing river dolphins and redfin mahseer. Its north bank offers an unrivalled view of the Taj.

There we met two Indian boys in their late teens. For several minutes they edged into my photos, giggling, and when I turned the lens directly on them, they gleefully did a walking-to-the-dance-floor dance and settled into lunging poses in front of me, grinning. The handsome one with the pencil moustache popped his hips and dropped his denim jacket off his shoulders to reveal a T-shirt which had 'If You Are Bad. I Am Your Dad..!' written on the front of it. The one with the dyed-red curtains rested one foot on a fence post and stared smoulderingly into the distance.

A couple of times obsessive doubts flared up – of the two boys getting off with each other, *was I into it?* – but sticking with the plan, I again tried to shrug them off by reminding myself of the loop tape's objective truths: *I don't have to be aroused by most men to be straight.*

Everything about these boys, from the metallic turquoise shirt to the Blue Steel expressions, was a reason to love this country. They smacked triumphantly of India's perpetual capacity to surprise and delight, to pull off the unlikely and the spectacular. Black satin flares? Why not. Platform trainers? Sure. 'If You Are Bad. I Am Your Dad . . . !' I don't know what that means, but it doesn't matter. Because India is visceral and bright and sensually exhilarating, and so unlike the polished white stone of its most famous monument, which gleams lifeless in profile pictures and travel brochures and Ikea picture frames the world over.

'Oh my God,' someone said, opening the curtains at dawn. We'd crossed the border into Nepal. Always the last one on the bus to get up, I scrambled from my blanket to see. Over the black Himalaya the air glowed a fleshy, translucent pink, and faded upwards with digital brilliance into the late midnight blue. A disco moon hung in the violet, flecking a million sparkling dots into space, its silverblack sphere unzipped at one side into a seductive crescent of dazzling white.

The tour guide drove us to the viewpoint up the mountain roads. At the hairpins you could see into the surrounding valleys, where the peaks of the lower range crowned like sharks' fins from a sea of thick mist.

Climbing the steps to the viewing platform, treading the earth-brown stones, I noticed, like you notice a passing plane, that I wasn't obsessing, and in noticing I disturbed a worryflutter in my chest. But it faded as we reached the peak and saw the last stars wink beyond the horizon to the other side of the world.

The crew stood huddled together. A couple of them now felt like real friends and I put my arms around them. We waited for the sun to rise.

An English family stood next to us – an ageing, podgy couple and their podgy teenage son, the most English people you ever saw. I watched them while we waited. I figured they must have thought they couldn't have kids until he was conceived some time in their mid forties, and he was the centre of their middle aged worlds. The boy was the exact blend of his parents. He had a shadow of mousy down on his face and he was wearing an awkward hiking outfit. Feet too big for his body. His voice was breaking. The way he looked at our group with shy eyes, the way his parents seemed to nod kindly without understanding the things he said, the way he agonised over what to do with his hands when he stood still, reminded me so much of my own adolescent perplexity. His mother's tight fitting beanie, which made her pink ears poke out over her glasses, broke my heart a little. I wondered if she picked him up from school wearing it. The boy tugged at her sleeve as the sun broke in the east and a murmur of awe arose from the watching tourists. We looked towards Everest.

These few minutes of simply noticing, of simply being absorbed by something other than myself, offered the comfort I'd been desperately seeking. *Maybe I've cured myself*, I whispered, as the first rays of the sun touched the snow-capped peaks in the west. *Maybe I'll actually have a good time at the beach festival.* Maybe the compulsive rationalisation of the loop tapes had worked. Maybe it'd finally succeeded in turning my identity into an unfettered, clear-cut thing. Unequivocal like the mountains.

Fifty Thousand Fatties

Pristine Western Australia. The smell of coconut lotion and fresh seafood cooked on public barbecues. The pock of golf balls on immaculate lawns and the roar of waves, watched closely by lifeguards in ironed polo shirts and unscratched sunglasses. Privilege gleamed on every surface as far as the eye could see.

I was due home in London in less than two weeks' time.

We parked near the beach and walked from the bus to the festival site, following the perimeter fences across dry grassland. I was ten shades paler than anyone for miles around and the sun was hot on my skin. We walked in a stream of hundreds. Hundreds of boys in board shorts and neon vests and panama hats. Hundreds of girls in denim hot pants and neon bikinis and panama hats. A river of tanned, toned flesh.

A couple of times anxiety swelled in my throat to see this cleavage or that ass. But I was determined not to trigger, and so far my doubts had been drowsy, like wasps at the end of summer. I'd had a few shots of ouzo on the bus before we left, and that'd helped, too.

'I'm better,' I whispered, as we approached the festival gates.

Once inside we headed straight for the dance tent where Metronomy were playing. I felt confident that their funky push-and-pull would keep my brain distracted from the crowd's bouncing boob buffet, and by the second track, the bass and the ouzo had me grinning.

The chorus of track three. I stopped dead, as the girl in front of me took her top off. My grin vanished. *No*, I thought, as I imagined licking the back of her neck.

I'm better.

I'm better.

I'm better.

But the compulsion didn't work and more thoughts buzzed into my mind – *lick her neck, lick her neck, lick her neck* – and I flinched from their stings. The band were playing 'The Bay', a song I adored and had many times played on my bass in my bedroom, badly, but with *so* much love. And even that couldn't overpower the doubts. By the end of the set the thoughts were swarming and I was spinning, eyes wide, imagining fifty thousand people naked.

Now I was noticing all the girls bobbing up and down on boys' shoulders. The words *fifty thousand fatties grinding fifty thousand necks* kept charging through my head and I tried to lessen their sting by singing them to the tune of Ten Green Bottles. But it didn't work. And on the crotches ground, all through Metronomy's encore. I crunched the beer can in my palm.

Next up, The Kooks. I wanted to leave but the lead singer's genital bulge had me transfixed, so tightly packed were his balls into a pair of skinny jeans. The ruminations started jabbering.

Am I turned on?

I looked at Kooks Man's balls, to check.

Oh, my God, not at all.

So does that mean I'm gay?

I looked back at the chub to check I wasn't aroused.

I didn't feel aroused.

If I'm not aroused maybe I'm gay.

No. I don't fancy him, that's all . . .

But if I was straight maybe I WOULD fancy him.

Maybe all the other girls here have got fat panties over him.

And even though I objectively knew that this entire internal conversation was preposterously irrational, the compulsive urge to rationalise was overwhelming, and I scanned the girls around me to see if they seemed aroused by Kooks Man's balls. I saw one girl kissing a boy.

Maybe she snogged him spontaneously because she was so turned on by Kooks Man's balls?

Maybe I should be turned on by balls, too?

Am I turned on by balls?

I looked at his crotch and tried really hard to be turned on. I wasn't turned on.

Fuck. Fuck. Fuck. I don't fancy him. I don't fancy him.

Maybe this proves I AM gay.

Am I?

No.

Am I?

No.

Am I?

No.

Am I?

No.

Am I?

No.

Am I?

No.

Am I?

No.

Am I?

'No!' I scream but no-one hears. I looked back at Kooks Man's balls and the kissing couple and back at Kooks Man's balls.

Maybe I'd prefer looking at a vagina squished into those jeans?

I imagined a vagina where Kooks Man's balls were, and focused all of my attention on my arousal levels. For a second I thought I felt a twinge.

Oh my God. Maybe that means I'm gay. And if I'm gay then I can't be with Toby.

Though I knew on some level that they weren't, the thoughts felt as real as ever. My breath started galloping into panic. And the panic, as panic tends to, made me panic more.

Am I panicking because I know it's true?

No, I'm panicking because I've got OCD.

I've got OCD.

I've got OCD.

I drew my attention to my chest, and tried to look deep inside myself, to try and figure out what my body was trying to tell me.

Maybe if I can stop panicking it'll prove that this isn't an identity crisis —I tried to slow my breathing but it quickened and quickened and quickened and I cut my palm on the crunched beer can in my hands, and without saying anything

I left the others and zigzagged through the crowd, looking at the ground—

A blond-haired teenager with 'cool as f*uck.' written on his T-shirt, all in lower case, full stop, crashed into me because he was moshing – no joke, *moshing* – to The Kooks, and then his friend, wearing a pink scoop neck vest that said 'GEEK' on it, put his arm around me and tried to make a moment happen by swaying me from side to side and shouting beery song lyrics into my face: 'Shine, shine, shine on, won't you shine, shine on,' but I brushed him off with a grimace—*Maybe the panic is the true 'me' trying to get out—no I'm panicking because I've got OCD—but if I DID have OCD it would be better by now—I've been doing everything the therapist said so I should be better—this should be gone by now—I should be better—I love Toby but I can't be with him—I can't live if I don't know who I am—*

At the back of the crowd by the sweet-sick-smelling portaloos I turned back to face the stage and stare into the strobe, not knowing why I'd run or where I was going or what I'd tell the others in the morning, and I stood with my two feet flat and unreal on the ground, as the whole world swooshed in blurs all around me. Then I did something that I'd never done before, I floated off, let myself go completely, imagined myself not alive. In the smoky haze, above this crowd full of beauties, I imagined my body hanging from the proscenium arch of the stage, swaying softly in the fading light. This was no intrusive thought. No obsession. No unwanted intrusion. This was desired, an indulgence, a square of chocolate in the mouth, a Müller advert. As the bodies bustled all around me, I stood still, watching the stage, wilfully suspending myself in that lifeless thought, then I vomited, and ran, and hid in my bunk all night.

Cut Crystal

The morning after the festival I blended in because everyone was hungover and lying down facing the windows. The rest of Australia was all in bits. Moving light glimpsed through the darkness of closed eyes. Just days to go until I was planning to fly home.

I thought about the paroxetine in my bag – the stuff I'd been prescribed in Paris. I thought it might make me feel better if I started taking it, but I was frightened. I didn't want to lose control surrounded by people I didn't know. Questions went round and round as the wheels of the bus made for Sydney.

Should I tell Toby I want to die?

Should I tell Toby I have OCD?

What if I told him I had OCD and then I realised that I *didn't*, and that this was all a lie? Hollywood said it's good to 'open up'. But what if you don't know what you're opening? How can you 'let people in' when you don't know what's inside?

For the following three days the outback stretched indefinitely in front of us like another world. In the Nullarbor Desert you could watch the hot snakes and scorpions crawling the red earth, seeking shade under the gnarled blue-greenery when the sun apexed in opaque sky. Dead kangaroos, first glimpsed dancing in the heatwaves, singed at the sides of the road. Being there and looking at horizons too distant to see, I knew Galileo was wrong. The world is flat, too flat to be round.

In trendy Fitzroy, Melbourne, we went out for pizza. After four months of on-the-road chitchat, conversation often turned polemical, and now it turned to suicide.

'It's the ultimate selfish act,' someone said.

'Yeah, I mean, everyone's got choices. And it's just totally unfair to choose to inflict that kind of pain on other people,' another added.

I'd been listening, reticent as usual, but now I could not keep quiet. 'I think that's simplistic,' I said.

'How so?'

'One of my best mates went through a suicidal episode. But she was ill. It had nothing to do with choice,' I said, testing them. 'To look at her you'd think she had everything – an awesome job which meant she could travel, a gorgeous boyfriend—'

'Nah, bull. You always have choices, *especially* if you're privileged. If my girlfriend was suicidal that'd be the biggest insult to me,' one of the guys said with a mouthful of pizza.

My stomach heaved. *I'm an insult.* 'I'm not sure you can really rationalise it like that,' I said.

'I'm sorry Rose, but you *can*. If you're in love with someone then that person should make you happy, end of.'

I waited for the subject to change before getting up and walking through the bar to the toilet, and with each step my eyes filled up a little more. I fiddled with the lock and closed the cubicle door behind me, resting both my palms flat against it and looking at the floor. A drop trickled down my nose and fell. Then another and another.

They were right. The feeling of not wanting to be alive falls so pathetically short of romance. 'Be always so young and in love' an Italian waiter had once said to Toby and I, as he upturned chairs all around us. I'd looked across the table through the unfurling candlesmoke and felt like we might be. But Death is Love's antithesis, surely? That's what we've always been told. 'There is no fear in love,' the Bible said. So my current feelings of extreme Love and extreme Fear were antithetical. My Self was a contradiction, an impossibility.

The following morning I sat alone on Circular Quay in Sydney, waiting for the train to take me to the airport for my plane to London. The Saturday wedding guests breezed down the quayside, tanned and beautiful in the blustery sun. Couples in pastels – apricot tulle and lavender silk – spread bright white smiles for snapshots by the cut-crystal water. Forever the white tiers of the Sydney Opera House will shine in the background of their mantelpiece photos, framed with swirls of silver. Nothing is sacred. As my mind had perverted my own ideals, so it perverted theirs, lifting up the taffeta gowns of their bridesmaids and bending ushers over bonnets.

These darlings inhabited another world. In 30 hours I'd be back in mine.

Part Three

Part Three

Jake Gyllenhaal

There's snow on the ground. It's past midnight and the world is a strange, milky yellow. The warehouses are black against the jaundiced sky and shrieks of snowballers can still be heard from the alleys. Here and there, cast iron staircases host precarious piles of snowflakes, and it is still snowing hard. My knuckles are dappled purple as they grip the cast iron balcony railing. I got back a week ago and I want to jump.

It started okay, better than okay. It started beautifully.

On the flight from Sydney I calculate exactly what time to apply my make-up in the plane bathroom, to make sure that I look as fresh as possible when I see Toby at the airport for the first time. An hour before landing I close the cubicle door behind me and set to work applying mascara, watching the brush tremble over my lashes in the mirror.

I'm distracted: I've just glimpsed a sex scene on the TV across the aisle from my seat, and the perky breasts of the Victoriana heroine are there in the reflection of my eyes as I quiver with the tar-slicked bristles. An impatient rap at the door and a black glob falls onto the bridge of my nose. *Shit.* I wipe it with toilet tissue and it smears across my face. I fumble, drop my mascara into the toilet bowl. *No! Shit!*

Now just one eye done, the other still pink and pale like a pig's eye, with sad, pale lashes.

Another rap at the door: 'There are people waiting out here.'

A woman's voice! I picture her tits. Big Victorian tits. Matron's tits. School-kid-fantasy tits. They are going to ruin it, I am sure. Now a tit is floating in the mirror. I press my index fingers against my lower lids to stop the black running.

Don't cry.

Don't cry.

Don't cry.

If there's one thing you don't need at an airport reunion it's a big haunting tit ghost all up in your face, swelling between you when you're gazing into each other's eyes; when he's gazing into your sad pig eye.

I go through customs and the Bluto-esque border official sneers at the embossed teeth marks on the corners of my passport, which I've held in my mouth countless times while scrabbling at the front of queues for forgotten documents. He almost vomits when a sprinkle of sand falls from the water-stained pages onto his marbled plastic counter, as if I've personally insulted Queen and country, insulted *him* as a man. I purse my lips, scared that the laboured *go fuck yourself* which is jabbering at him from inside my head will burst out and get me arrested. As he slams down the stamp with a huff, a small bead of saliva pops from his red, red lips, and in a flash they begin to suckle at the giant floating tit, like a kid goat on a teat.

In years to come I will reflect on OCD's awesome levelling power – its ability to indiscriminately reduce humans to their basest and their most vulnerable. I will love it for triumphing over the little enemies of day to day – the jobsworths and the queue-skippers and youths who let old ladies stand on the tube – all have succumbed to the mighty tit and willy, their pomposity quite literally pricked.

But today, as Bluto is lovingly nursed by the giant mam, such appreciation is unthinkable.

It's going to ruin it, I think.

Customs cleared. I start along the grey corridors and the trolley wheels squeak in front of me. Around each blind corner Toby might be waiting. But ten or more corners reveal nothing. Just the sleep-ruffled heads of the other arri-vees. And the tit ghost, once or twice. I breathe quick. Pick my cuticles. Fluff my hair.

Then the light comes round the bend and I see him standing in the big terminal's brightness in front of the gate, wearing the bobble hat he'd put on with childlike pride the day he bought it. He sees me straight away because he's watching everyone coming out, and I catch the start of a deep beam spreading across his face. He is tall and beautiful and I feel lovely as he puts his arms around me. We say nothing but press our lips together – not kissing, just touching lips and holding each other tight through our thick coats. His weasely fur-trimmed parka tickles my face. I flick a tear from the end of his nose and we break into smiles, pressing our foreheads together and mouthing little 'hellos' between kisses, proper kisses now, I love you kisses, I can't believe you did that to me kisses, I missed you kisses.

That hurt so fucking much kisses.

And then we stand very still and hug for a long time before walking to the station.

We sit close on the train and the winter sun flickers through the tower blocks of Hatton and Hounslow. We are self-conscious. There are people sat opposite us in the carriage. They are looking at my bags and at us, at my tan, and the way his hand rolls over mine, at the way he rediscovers my fingernails with tiny strokes, at the way I trace the grain of his hair from his temples down to his jaw. They see these things and they know that I've been away and that we're in love. And because we hate couples like us, we try not to touch too much, but it doesn't work and we keep creasing into shy, unstoppable kisses. This is the start kisses.

The towns rush past the window, brown and cold and bright and familiar. I watch them and he watches me. I'm wondering if he's wondering if I'm better. I'm wondering what I'll say if he asks.

When we get home he shoulders my bag up the stairs and lays me on the bed and strokes my hair, which I know is lying out behind me on the pillow, all wavy like in the ads. I stretch my arms and make cubbish noises and make myself more tired and delicate than I really am, because he is relishing being able to look after me, and because I am relishing giving myself over to him. We *loathe* couples like us.

He lies down next to me and we look at each other. We hold each other at arm's length and pull each other close, we squint and we widen our eyes, trying to look at this unseeable feeling from other angles. There's a lot of 'ssshhing' and twice that night I cry when the obsessions come – the tit ghost, and a thought of the festival. But the love is bigger. Nothing has ever been bigger than them but now the love is a giant and they are tiny. They are scanty and pitiful and cowering beneath this thing that roars between us when we kiss. Now there is a stillness, like the blissful-deep moment an incessant alarm stops.

But this present is a suspension, an ellipsis, a holiday. I know that when the jetlag excuse wears off, I'll have to be a part of the world again. Toby will open the curtains, play DVDs, suggest walks in the park and meals in restaurants, and the OCD will rise like an animal disturbed from sleep, snapping and spitting inside me.

It happens sooner than I thought it would – that weekend, when I meet the girls for the first time since getting back from the trip.

Our friend is producing a music video and she's invited us to be extras on the shoot. It's a nightclub scene and the director wants it to look as naturalistic as possible, so we just have to get pissed and dance. It's pretty much a standard night out, but with free drinks and Jake Gyllenhaal.

Gyllenhaal is the star of the video, playing a hipster-hating serial killer who rampages through the basement clubs and warehouse parties of east London, slitting the throats and breaking the necks of flannel-wearing, Raybanned dickheads – dickheads who dance like morons and drug themselves stupid and pose for selfies. In this scene Gyllenhaal maintains a face of deadpan disdain as he walks through an over-excited dance floor crowd, thinking murderous thoughts.

We'd been asked to wear our most trendy clothes, and unless the whole club has taken their commitment to their costumes so far as to get their hair cut accordingly, I'm guessing most of us didn't have to delve too deep into our wardrobes to find something appropriate. The self reflexive irony is not lost on anyone, except maybe the *really* extreme cases – the people with the vintage Versace shirts and Dali moustaches and swallow tattoos and undercuts; the people so cutting edge they cut the edge off their better judgment and rendered themselves blunt through their obtuse and aching trendiness.

But most of us recognise the awkward truth which sits in the air with the Tom Ford White Patchouli and swirls like smoke in the strobe: the aesthetic of fashionable vacuousness and asininity which has been created here tonight is being played out without parody in every other club within half a mile – clubs we'd all be in if we weren't here, with free drinks and Jake Gyllenhaal. Who cares if the joke's on us. Even the most nonchalant extra will, in months to come, casually drop into conversation that they were 'there'. And that's what makes the resulting video so knowing and so brilliant.

I should be enraptured to be here. All the girls and gay men are frothing their pants over the prospect of being this close to Gyllenhaal, talking about his angel's bow, about his pecs, about what they'd do to him given the chance, about who-cares-if-he's-not-skinny-anymore, about his blue, blue eyes – 'omigod SO blue' – and his perpetual bed hair.

I smile and nod but I'm not listening. Below the eye line of the crowd I'm working on my cuticles until they bleed, because this whole club is naked and grinding up against me. Each time the director shouts 'ACTION' over the music and Gyllenhaal starts making his way across the dance floor, I see each pouted lip, each thrust pelvis, each cat-like over-shoulder glance. I miss nothing. They are all assigned roles: you the taker, you the giver, you the bender, you the bendee, you the gurner, you the squealer. People in sequins dance past me, grinning. I should be alight and ablaze, but my obsessions are sucking up the oxygen.

Still. Fuck! *Still*, even now, I'm wondering if maybe I got the whole OCD thing wrong. *Maybe my identity is a lie.* Still, when the images come they feel like real life challenges. Still they're telling me that my life and my love is a sham. Still, even though I know rationally that they're irrational. Still, after everything I've learned about the tricks and fibs of the doubting disease; after discovering that millions like me have thoughts like mine; after all the age-old romance and all the fantasies about my future with Toby, *still* the doubts are razing my sense of self to the ground. Only now, I feel, as I shuffle my feet on the sticky floor in this demented Dalston basement, there's not much left to raze.

'ACTION.'

This is a moment! A shining, youthful moment. Here the silverscreen superstar. Here the beautiful people. Here the cameras and the drugs and the shimmering skin and the Jamesons, all caught up in this one hedonistic distillation. Now Gyllenhaal is standing right next to me, facing me. This is crystalline, this is Hollywood, right here. He looks at me and our eyes meet and his whole face is a chubby vagina, a vagina Cyclops, a giant, dancing vagina.

I stand still and do a little gasp but the music's too loud for anyone to hear. Seeing me motionless, one of the girls takes my hand and spins me round and round. As we pirou-ette the spotlights stream in my vision, whooshing against the dark, tightening their rings around me, whisking euphoria into menace. *This is not how I'm supposed to feel.* Not now. Not on this night. Not in Hollywood.

Then a Daft Punk track comes on and the whole club starts marching and pouting to the solid four beat bars, progressing somewhere without me. Someone's vogueing cause vogueing's back in. The running man is definitely not, but someone's giving that a go, anyway. Glasses are raised. Fingers point to the ceiling. People don't know the lyrics but they pretend that they do. I try to get inside the moment with force. I put on these huge smiles and pretend to laugh and pout. I try to grab the moment by the throat, pin it down and make it yield. But the more I thrash the further it flees. My friend lets go of my hand as she turns to greet someone, and we stop spinning. I stand still, impotent, and through the dizziness the thoughts come hammering. The vagina-face and the tit ghost and the Russian millionaire and Ten Green Bottles—

I race the sticky stairs, holding the handrails tight. I stand in the club doorway and hesitate before the bouncer asks me 'Are you in or out?'

'Out.'

I step onto the pavement and the cold snaps. In the street more cameras shoot snowball fights. The cameramen are encouraging people to act like morons, and they rush past me laughing and grunting. One boy knocks my bag from my hand, sending my lipstick and wallet clattering to the gritty-wet pavement amid the sludge and fags.

'Oh my God, *honey,* I'm so sorry.' A boy with swallow tattoos and an undercut puts a hand on each of my shoulders, before diving to pick up my things. 'I'm so sorry, babe.

Are you okay?' he asks, looking at the scuffs on my wallet, placing my things in my hands. Then he looks into my face and asks, in a different way, about a different thing, 'Oh, babes, are you *okay*?' His palms are warm and he is lovely.

I don't say anything. I turn from him and shuffle away from the club, sludging my feet in the snow, which is so cold and so grey—

Shut up. Fuck. Who else would call it 'grey'?

I prejudged that boy and he was lovely. Never mind swallow tattoos and undercuts and Versace shirts and Instagram. Never mind. Never mind. Never mind.

Who fucking cares?

These people are young and positive and beautiful, just kids on mufti day, wanting to be loved, wanting to be a part of something bigger. That's all there is to say. That's all there has *ever* been to say. My cynicism doesn't raise me up. I am not clever. A therapist once said that I intellectualised my life to hide from it, and she was right. It's easier to pick holes in a moment than admit that it's just *you* who's not having a good time. It's easier to sneer at Facebook than it is to change the way you think about it. It's easier to construct shabby satires than be earnest. It's easier to be snide about the choices of others than it is to stare down your own unhappiness. What awkward truth? What fucking *irony*?

I am so small and so sad. I walk the squealing streets below the groups of girls arm in arm, catching snowflakes on their tongues; below the boys, be-beanied and boisterous, concealing snowballs in their palms; below the couples – perfect *Kooples* couples – admiring their footprints behind them.

Do I tell Toby?

I imagine his head in his hands, his this-is-too-much face, me standing alone with my big bag in the lamp-lit street.

Or do I not?

I could just freeze right here on the grey ice—

—*Shut up, shut up, shut up.*

I walk up the stairs of Toby's building, thinking about how high his balcony is from the ground, and about those pills from Paris that I still have in my stuff somewhere. I put the key in the lock and turn it slowly.

Chubby Pocket

Toby must've gone out for a drink because he's not here. I step away from the balcony and go back inside. Then I go back outside. Then back inside again.

The anxiety comes in leagues-deep lunges. Like contractions. I search for the tablets.

How many would I have to take?

Twenty? Fifty?

What would it look like?

Vomiting? Fits?

So dismal and predictable.

Another contraction.

I could just jump.

'Hello love,' Toby says, walking into the room. I hadn't heard the key in the lock. I don't say anything.

He chats as he takes off his coat and finds somewhere to put his keys. He hasn't looked at me properly yet. 'You've Lennied it in here—' he starts saying, stepping over the contents of my bag strewn across the floor, but stops when he looks at my face properly, and rushes to me.

'Heeey . . . ?' I sit up. I raise my eyelids from the bed, to the wall, to his hands, to his face. He takes me by the shoulders. 'What's the matter?'

I look at him and blink but don't say anything.

'Rose.' He never calls me that. 'What's the matter? I thought you were at the shoot?'

'I left.' I must say it fatally because his worry becomes feverish.

'Rose, look at me.'

I look at my lap and shake my head and say little no's.

'Shhhh,' he says, changing tactic, stroking my hair, 'What is it?'

'Nothing.'

'Rose?'

'Nothing, I just felt really bad tonight—'

'Okay,' he says pragmatically. And then I can't say anything for a long time, and he rocks me, waiting until I can.

'I wanted it all to be perfect,' I eventually say, 'and it's been so amazing being back here with you–but–it's hard–when I get really, really bad–when I get *this* bad—' I put my hand against my mouth but he takes it away—'sometimes I think I want to die.' Somehow this is easier to say than the other, darker OCD secret. He nods and swallows but his tears come straight away, making mine stop. 'Like tonight. For the past hour I've just been seeing myself die over and over again. I keep thinking about the tablets in the bottom of the bag and the balcony and stuff.'

I feel cruel because I can't look at him crying, and I know that he needs me. I lie back down on the bed.

He doesn't say anything for many seconds but I can hear his deep breathing, in and out, and then one huge breath before he speaks again.

'You're thinking about the pills in the bag?' he says, shaking.

I nod.

'Right,' he says.

He goes over to my bag and starts rummaging, pulling out clothes with a force that startles me. His mouth is tight. He pulls out a pill box and drops it on the floor, then another, then another. The pale orange light from the lampshade stretches tiny soft-grey shadows of braille across the boxes' white cardboard. He breathes deep as he scoops the boxes from the floor, and clutches them to his chest. He lets them fall on the mattress next to me and they click like eggs. He looks at me, still shaking, and gestures towards the tablets '. . . so you don't have to think about them in the bottom of the bag anymore. So you don't have to worry on your own about them down there.' He can barely speak for crying, now. 'Because they're here now, and I'm with you, and they're not going to hurt you.'

'I'm so sorry,' I say, touching the back of his neck.

'I've got something else to show you.' He pulls away and starts to laugh with a touch of hysteria, reaching for the shelf behind him. I sink lower into the bed as I watch him, and the duvet fuzzes out of focus in my fore-vision. A shadow of a blade flashes on the wall and he comes to me with it cupped in his palm.

'Here,' he says, placing the fishing knife on the bed.

I don't look at it.

'Here!' he says, placing it on my chest. He curls my fingers around the metal blade and holds his hands around mine, on my belly. I can feel the coldness through my cotton vest and his pulse racing in his arms.

'It's okay.' He squeezes my hands as he says it. 'These things cannot hurt you. You don't have to be afraid of them on your own.'

He is trying to be strong, but I see what I am taking from him. I see that my secret, untreated condition is draining him dry, because the life into which he's pouring himself has a hole in it.

I breathe deep and close my eyes. An electric green smudge buzzes and flickers and fades in the black noise under my lids. I have to tell him. On a thousand nights, over years and years, I've drifted with the phosphene stars in the darkness of my closed eyes, imagining what I was about to say – the words and intonation of a lifetime's secret I never believed I'd tell; imagining the reaction of a lover whose face I didn't yet know. I open my eyes and he's watching me, calmer now, stroking his thumb over my fingers which clutch the blade. I feel the drawn air push against the inside of me. My mouth feels heavy as I open it.

'I see sexual images in my mind.' It comes out small. He stops stroking my fingers and pauses momentarily, then, recollecting himself and not wanting me to see his surprise, squeezes my hand with an encouraging 'Okay . . .'

I can't look at him as I go on. 'When I'm walking down the street or watching TV or something, I see people naked. It's really graphic—' I speak into the cotton volume of the duvet, which seems to absorb my words and make them safer. He is quiet for five hour-long seconds.

'And the thoughts scare you?' He strokes my hand.

'Yeh.' A tiny word.

'Why do they scare you, love?'

I still can't look at him. Can't even speak, now.

'Love?' he asks again.

'I'm scared about what they might mean.'

'What they might mean . . .' he pauses, thinks about his

words. My stomach flexes. I reel inside. It's too embarrassing, too deeply-buried, too secret, and the quick of me curls like a salted slug. *I have sinned in my own thoughts. I have sinned in my own thoughts. I have sinned in my own thoughts. I have sinned in my own thoughts—*

'. . . about your sexuality?' he says, completely unfazed.

I gape at him. *Maybe he understands.*

'Yeh. It's like obsessive, OCD stuff. I know my thoughts don't make any sense but I can't stop thinking them.'

I press my face against the pillow. But he won't let me lie there feeling ashamed. He takes the fishing knife and the pill boxes from my chest and lays them on the pillow next to me. He slides a hand between the small of my back and the mattress, and the other behind my head, as though it'd bend like a baby's if he didn't. Then he draws me towards his chest. I exhale deeply as I let my body rest against the strength of his arms. Snapped sobs tremble my back as he coos at me, as if to a puppy scared by thunder.

'Shhh.' He kisses my temple. 'It's okay.' I raise one limp arm and rest a hand on his chest. His heart is beating quick. 'So I guess that means you're always trying to kind of figure it out?'

Oh my God, he DOES understand. I nod.

He holds me for a long time until I stop crying. Then he shakes his head and grins. 'That explains your hardcore gay porn collection then.'

'Oh Tobe,' I cringe. He smacks my arse.

'I found it on your laptop when we first started going out. Thought you were just a little perve.'

We giggle, me weakly.

'Oh HEY . . .' he says, smacking my arse again, having an

idea. 'I saw this guy on a chat show once – I can't even remember who it was but it was someone famous – and he was talking about this time he got a little involuntary semi when he was play-fighting with his mate . . .' Toby gets distracted for a second by the wobble of my ass.

'And . . . ?' I say, as the anxiety rises in my throat again.

'. . . And it proper weirded him out, because he was a straight guy and had a wife and stuff, and it'd never happened before. And he kept on ruminating about it, trying to figure out if he'd been turned on. Then a few days later a cat jumped on his lap and gave him another chubby pocket. And he was laughing about it, saying he never thought there'd come a day when he'd be pleased to get a boner over a domestic animal.'

'God, sounds familiar.' We giggle a few moments more, but then he stops me and is serious again. He turns my head so I'm looking straight into his eyes.

'Thank you for trusting me with that.'

'I trust you with everything,' I say, lying back down on the bed.

Above me there is a poster of woodland creatures, ripped at the bottom corners from where we've done shoulder stands up the wall. Tucked into the poster's edge is a postcard from Goa. The sea is as blue as I remember.

'We're going to sort this out, love, don't worry. We'll find the people who can help you. It doesn't matter where we have to go or how much it costs, we'll just make it work, I promise.' His voice is deep and the lamplight is soft, and for the first time in a very long time, being alive is quiet and beautiful.

Betty Boop

I choose a world-renowned OCD therapy centre in New York. I'm due to have Skype sessions once a week for however long it takes. I don't know whether it'll be better than the other therapies I've experienced, *endured*, but I've gotta gamble. Things have never been more fucked. I am at the apex of fuckery and if I fall this time – I don't know, *I don't know – je suis fuckée*.

Telling Toby was a brief relief, no doubt, but no panacea. *What was I thinking?* That him knowing would change something fundamental about my neurology? 'A problem shared is a problem halved?' Bullshit. The global story bias has no truck with the grinding tenacity of mental illness: when was the last time you saw a drawn-out soap opera storyline in which someone spent *years* bottling something up before finally mustering the strength to confide in a loved one, and then literally NOTHING CHANGED?

The therapy sessions are £100 a pop and I can't afford it. So I make money writing bullshit for bullshit web start-ups with bullshit concepts – mobile-hive-swapping and digital-data-hounding and social-data-hive-crowd-mapping – which will make someone a lot of money but which are dry and bodiless. The bullshittiest gig of all is writing self-help content for a media behemoth.

Self. Help.

On a typical morning I get out of bed in tears and eat brie straight off the block, before sitting down in the dark to write a 1000-word piece of life-advice called 'Be Successful' or 'Make Friends Easily' or 'Achieve Job Satisfaction'. At the height of its popularity the resulting e-book is downloaded 15,000 times a day. When I read a trumpeting email from my boss telling me that my job role now has an official title, I sit in my knickers laughing blackly, spraying clods of short-bread at the screen. I grab my phone to text Jack: 'FYI, I am now officially a "Life Coaching Editor".'

But despite my professional whoring, the £400-a-month therapy bill renders me more skint than I've ever been, and I revel in it, delectably traipsing the aisles of the Turkish mart downstairs and counting out the change on the counter. One day they give me some BBQ Beef Hula Hoops on credit and I am thrilled. I don't know why. I guess physical discom-fort offers a concrete-and-upright worry amid the mental dereliction.

The first session is at 7pm tonight, and I've decided I should make an effort with my appearance. I came to this decision yesterday morning. I'd gone to Tesco in men's grey jogging bottoms, hot pink fleece (with misc. stains), tailored navy pea coat, and the first pair of shoes I found at the door: smart black Chelsea boots with a midi-heel. I caught my reflection in a window on the way back from the till. The bulkiness of my fleece made my shoulders two feet wide and the boots were barely visible under the bulge of the too-long trackies. I was standing with my heels together and my feet at ten-to-two, and I'd wrapped a bobbly scarf around my neck, on top of my hair, which'd now loosened and turned my head into a perfect wide-bottomed triangle.

'I look fucking mental,' I said, already down to the crotch of a Dairy Milk Freddo.

But today I am trying not to look mad, because the stuff I am about to say out loud to a complete stranger is off-the-scale, bat-shit-crazy. Hair is brushed and I settle for a plain black crew neck and blue jeans, and put on a watch for some reason, even though I already know that it's exactly 6.17pm. Today I am dusting down my polished outer self. It is measured and consistent and reliable like the cogs in a ticking clock. Today I am a good citizen.

I consider which corner of my bedroom to host the call. My white sheets have gone all saggy and grey, and the duvet is bunched up into a sorry ball in the bottom of its sack. On the shelf above the headboard a yoghurt pot sits inside a Kronenburg pint glass, which in turn sits inside a Sports Direct mug, among several screwed-up tissues and an empty can of coke. So I discount the bed area, settling instead for the settee-come-clothes-horse, which just needs a couple of weeks' mechanical excavation to make it presentable.

Then it's 6.45pm and everything is ready, and I'm sitting there on my bare settee with my laptop on the table in front of me, fully charged. And as I watch the minutes rise I wring my hands, which for the first time today have nothing to do. I pick up a compact mirror and fuss with my parting and practise my 'hello'. 6.54pm. Looking at my tired face I am struck for the first time today by the enormity of what's ahead. It's been 11 years since the night in the wood with the dog. How is anyone going to begin to fix that? Why should I believe that anyone can?

*

I cry about two minutes into the call and I'm not sure why. My therapist is pretty, that's for sure – brown hair and olive skin and an American accent which makes her seem like a star. *What if I've got the hots for her? What if I can't get any therapy done because I can't figure out whether or not I fancy her?* But I think I'm crying more out of relief. Or embarrassment? Who knows. When I describe one of my recent obsessions (imagining the owner of the shop downstairs banging one of the ladies from the launderette with a Fanta can) and she asks me to repeat it because there was a crackle on the line, it strikes me that this is one of the strangest situations I've found myself in.

My therapist knows all about me because I've already done an assessment to make sure I actually do have OCD and that I'm not making the whole thing up, though even now, as she talks, I'm obsessing about the possibility that maybe I *have* just lied my way here. Then I'm telling her about my previous therapies – about New Rose and Romanian orphanages – and though she is very professional and diplomatic, I see the scepticism in her eyes. When I say that in my last therapy I was asked to 'challenge my irrational beliefs' she stops me, eyebrow raised:

'Excuse me?'

'I had to rationalise my irrational doubts and tell myself that it wouldn't be 100% bad if I was gay.' And just for a second her composure falters and she shakes her head ever so slightly.

And when I notice that I've noticed this body language nuance of hers, I start doubting afresh:

Maybe I only noticed her little head shake because I'm staring at her.

Am I staring? I reshuffle my body compulsively and a sensation in my back makes me think that maybe I'm sub-consciously trying to stick my chest out.

What if I'm trying to turn her on?

What if she can tell *that I fancy her?*

Fuck, I don't *fancy her.*

But the fact I'm even questioning it might mean I do.

Am I staring at her?

This all happens as half-thoughts in about three seconds, and when I zone back in she's explaining something which sounds important, about how there's a lot of misinformation out there and a lot of unhelpful therapy, about the relation-ship between obsessions and compulsions, and how compul-sions make obsessions worse. And even though I'm now getting distracted by mental images of her naked and my anxiety is making it hard to think straight, so to speak, what she's saying seems to make sense, a *lot* of sense, more sense than anything any therapist has *ever* said.

'Compulsions make obsessions worse,' she's saying, 'that's the most important thing you'll learn during therapy. They just keep the vicious cycle of OCD spinning and spinning and spinning, which may be why you haven't seen any improvement in your condition over the years. So over the next few weeks we're going to start breaking down that vicious cycle, and you're going to start resisting the urge to act out compulsions. Is this making sense, Rose?'

It kind of *is* making sense, I think. I mean, it's not *all* new info. I already knew that obsessions and compulsions were different things – that obsessions were intrusive thoughts and compulsions were any attempt to escape or rationalise those thoughts – and my last therapist had already explained the cyclical nature of OCD. But I've never heard it expressed quite so simply. I nod, half-understanding what she's saying, though not yet fully realising its hugeness.

For homework I have to make a list of all the situations and things which scare me most. I also have to score each one out of ten, according to how anxious it makes me, ten being acute panic, one being just kinda 'meh'. There are no ones, twos or threes.

Weighing in at four is Facebook – a minefield for an obsessive. Not so much now, but a few years ago when professional stakes were lower, waistlines were slimmer, and need for external validation was higher, 'seductive' bedroom selfies were a regular feature of a casual newsfeed browse.

Coming in at five is fashion magazines, because there's a chance of actual tits, spesh if we're talking about your *i-D*s and your *Dazed & Confused*s. If ever I see one such publication on someone's coffee table I *have* to flick through and I *have* to make sure that I've checked every single image while monitoring my feelings – though I know it's an irrational and thoroughly flawed exercise, the compulsion is irresistible.

Sitting neck and neck at six are nightclubs, for instances of amateur erotic dancing, 'Any *Single Ladies* in the house toniiiiiiite?'; and gossip sites, whose dual agenda of titillating the blokes and shaming the birds proffers a daily spread of near-naked ladies. Spread being the operative word.

What does a six feel like? It'd change your breathing and swell your throat, and maybe have you sitting in the toilet with your head in your hands. Sixes are hourly occurrences at the moment – pretty much cruising speed.

Hotting up with number seven: music videos. Men in suits, women in bikinis. Men grabbing their crotches through baggy jeans, women rubbing theirs up imaginary poles. Men simulating pleasuring themselves, women simulating pleasuring men. The disproportionate female-male flesh ratio is particularly unhelpful for the sexuality obsessive.

At eight is watching films. A film could easily take out a whole day or a whole week if I'd seen something particularly graphic that just wouldn't shift. If I sense a sex scene coming on – when the actors are doing that weird sexy-eating crap or that weird sexy-fighting crap where they're throwing each other about and their hair's all scruffy – I'm already acting out anticipatory compulsions. Sometimes I'm already focusing all of my attention on my arousal levels. Sometimes I'm already watching the upcoming sex scene in my head. While the actors are licking away at their spoons like morons, my mind is already undressing them and taking them to bed. *How is this going to make me feel?* I ask myself. I remember once I was watching *Titanic* on Christmas Day and I knew the nude scene was coming up, so I screwed up my fists under my dressing gown and focused really, really, really hard on whether or not I was turned on, pouring all of my attention into my pants. So that when Kate Winslet reclined on the chaise longue and revealed her considerable mams, and the inevitable twinge came, it amounted to an irrefutable piece of evidence that my heterosexual life was a lie. Merry Freaking Christmas. The impression that moment scored in my brain was so deep that whenever I saw a brocade chaise longue in future, I'd picture that nude scene again, and retest my arousal levels afresh. Because every obsessive thought carves a groove in your mind, so that future thoughts roll along them with terrifying inevitability, like ball bearings, deepening the groove and rumbling through your brain for decades. Now the mere sight of a DVD makes my mind foam. It's Pavlovian.

At nine is the gym changing room, which naturally carries a high minge-risk.

The tens include The Beach, Strip Clubs, Lesbian Porn and Music Festivals. The latter may surprise you, seeing as full nudity is a statistical improbability at these events. But quantity trumps quality here – it's the sheer *number* of bodies at these things that's the problem, hence my Pig Pen freak out and my regrettable encounter with Kooks Man's balls. Putting obsessives in a festival and asking them not to act out compulsions is like locking alcoholics in a distillery and asking them not to drink. Every summer when the media shouts FESTIVAL SEASON, we go running, like pheasants scattering at the first autumn guns.

Next session we'll start these exposures. I won't be able to *physically* place myself in some of the situations – actual lesbian sex, for example, is off the menu – but they can be simulated with videos and images, which do a good enough job of triggering anxiety.

In contrast to the Flooding I'd done before going on the trip, when I'd gone from 0-60 in a heartbeat by asking out women on the street, these exposures will gradually increase in explicitness over many months, so that I can gradually habituate to the sexuality doubts and resulting anxiety.

My usual compulsive urge while doing these new thera-peutic exposures, of course, will be my standard body-scan: to analyse every thought in my head and tingle in my body, wringing them endlessly for an answer. Or to revert to one of the many compulsive mantras I've used over the years – 'It means nothing', 'I'm definitely gay', 'I'm having an OCD thought', etc. – which had attempted to concretely, inflexibly, *finally*, define my sexual identity.

But I will not be allowed. I will simply have to accept that my sexual identity *might* be in crisis. Over the next God-knows-how-long I will wade into each of my exposure situations doughy and limp, letting whatever thoughts happen, *happen* – letting them wash over me, unresisted and unconcluded.

That's the essential difference between the compulsive exposure I've engaged in myself over the years (*Attitude* and *Diva*, *The Story Of O*, Titgate, etc.) and the therapeutic exposure I'm engaging in now. The first had been an exercise in answer-seeking. The second is an exercise in accepting that there simply may not be any answers.

All humans have a compulsive tendency to analyse and explain and look for meaning in their thoughts, but the less attention we pay our thoughts generally, my therapist has explained, the less likely they are to become problematic.

I find this revelation surprising, given that my previous therapist had told me to work on my 'beliefs' everyday by repeating key phrases: 'if I was gay then it wouldn't be the worst thing in the world,' 'if I was gay I would be able to cope,' etc. Surely that had amounted to 'paying attention to my thoughts'?

She continues to work with utmost professionalism and still will not get drawn in to criticising her peers. But without directly calling anyone out, she says that yes, sadly, many therapists merely collude in and even encourage their patients' compulsive soul-searching, and that yes, it might be wise to discount much of what I've learned in previous courses.

For now she reckons that four is too high a level for me to start on, and I agree, so we take it down a notch and start with cartoons, which is when I feel most pathetic, when I slump down after the session and don't get up for hours because an amateur pencil sketch of a naked Betty Boop, drawn by some sex-starved virgin far away, has made me cry.

Life Coaching Editor. Fuck yeah.

Soon we'll move on to more hardcore stuff like pictures of *actual* women's faces(!!!), which I'll have to look at three, four, five times a day, reeling off a little script: 'maybe I'd enjoy kissing her', 'maybe I'd enjoy stroking her face', 'if I feel any sensations in my body it might mean I'm gay,' etcetera. Then we'll gradually look at more and more explicit images, and the script will increase in explicitness, too, right up to 'maybe I'd like to have sex with her' and 'maybe I'd like to shag her with a ten-inch', but that's pretty advanced stuff – sexual pandemonium, utter havoc, and right now I don't feel like I'll ever get there.

But I will. I'll be a diligent student. Eventually, towards the end of therapy, I'll jam my computer up with so much smut I'll bring it to its knees. In a gold star-worthy performance I'll watch so much porn I'll be able to identify the production company by the luxuriance of the pubic muffs, or lack thereof. I don't know how I'll get there but I'll try.

She-Ra

'Excuse me, boss, I'm just popping to the loo to read *Razzle*.'

There is no easy way of integrating exposure therapy into your professional routine. It requires planning. Every morning you're a new parent fretting about the baby bag, knowing that if you forget the blanket and the bottles all hell's gonna break loose at some point. Only my checklist is a little less cuddly, and before work at this or that ad agency I have to prepare for the day with certain questions. Will I get a morning break for exposure number one? Will the WiFi work in the toilets? Will I be sat next to someone who'll notice my trembling? What if someone uses my laptop and finds the smut file?

Mortifying. All of it.

The whole therapy-on-Skype thing is pretty awkward, too, given my paper-thin bedroom walls and the mouse-like demeanour of my sweet and kind French housemates. Every Monday evening before the session I put on the washing machine in the kitchen next door so that when they come home they won't hear me over its whirring – won't hear the throes of yet another boob-induced panic attack as they chow down on their tartes-aux-whatevers. I wash heavy denim items with buckles and rivets, for their superior clatter.

Toby's the only person who knows what the therapy involves. I've told my parents that I'm speaking to a therapist but I haven't gone into specifics. Things are more manageable now and the urgency to be 'saved' by them, or anyone else, for that matter, has waned. Besides, I could never quite imagine a way of bringing it up: 'Today I looked at ten whole tits, aren't you proud, Pops?'

Toby understands exactly what I have to do. Not that I talk him through each task or show him any of the materials – too. fucking. embarrassing. – but he gets it, totally, and sometimes when he's round my house I have to send him out of the room so I can catch a quick snippet of sexy. He'll boil the kettle twice if he needs to. It's a discreet system which works well enough to spare my cringes.

Until one day, about halfway through my therapy, the system fails.

I'm sat on the sofa having just done an exposure exercise – an *FHM* girl wearing only a tie, hat and glasses, as one does – and Toby's just come back into the room bearing cups of tea. He rests my mug on the coffee table, and takes the other with him to the bed, where he sits, and, without thinking, pulls my laptop onto his lap. I watch in slow mo as he opens it and the screen's blue-white light falls across his face, and with a bolt I realise. *OH GOD NO! HE'S SEEN THE EXPOSURE SCRIPT.* I'd left it maximised, the words I've just said to myself while gazing upon a near-naked lady, something about maybe wanting to kiss her tits or something. *OH GOD NO!* He shakes off his surprise and very sweetly minimises the window, not wanting me to know that he knows.

But it's too late, I saw it.

I run into the kitchen and start furiously washing up. He comes up behind me, saying, 'Oh love, don't be embarrassed, it's fine,' and tries to cuddle me. But I peel myself free and tell him to go away. Why? *Why* am I so embarrassed when he knew about the exposures already? I don't know – there's just something so, so, pathetic and so, so secret about all of this stuff.

Back in my bedroom I press my face into the duvet and won't look him and just say 'no' every time he tries to tell me it's okay, that it's no surprise. But for me there is a huge difference between him *knowing* it and him *seeing* it, an immeasurable difference. He says he understands, and softly leaves me alone when I ask. And I love him so much but it's not okay. What kind of wracked-off crackpot has to do this shit? Nothing about *any* of this is okay.

After about an hour, my hot face has cooled. I've had time to put things into perspective. As much as it felt it at the time, my embarrassment doesn't now seem absolutely, completely, *irrecoverably*, 100% bad. (Turns out that when applied to day-to-day niggles – rather than to OCD – the old 'awfulising' therapy stuff is actually very usual.) I get off the bed and walk over to the sofa and sit on Toby's lap.

He kisses me. I look him in the eyes. Then we burst out laughing.

On the advice of my therapist I've also started doing in-the-moment exposures in response to obsessive doubts. So if there's a cute receptionist at an agency and I feel an anxious lump rise in my throat, instead of trying to wriggle free of my anxiety with problem solving, I stare the anxiety in the face: *'maybe I DO fancy her,'* I tell myself. And then I just let the anxiety and the doubt wash over me, without acting out compulsions.

This is what my therapist calls a 'therapeutic response', and I do it all the time now, finding that the more I do it, the quicker the anxiety seems to go away. And already, looking back at the cartoony images I did at the beginning of the course, I don't feel as anxious.

But how could something that triggered me just a couple of months ago now pose no threat? How is the therapy working? For the answer we've got to scoot back a few millennia to the days of Stig of the Dump and Raquel Welch. Anxiety served a very useful function for early humans – it readied our bodies for fight or flight in the face of real bodily danger. The cavepeeps who didn't respond anxiously to a flash of fur in the bushes didn't live to pass on their genes. Those that *were* shit-scared enough to take action avoided death and so had their anxiety validated.

This feedback loop was so intense it endured the ages, and today OCD riffs off it. When people with the disorder have an obsessive fear – 'am I going to get eaten by a tiger?' – and respond by acting out a compulsion – 'I MUST DO EVERYTHING I CAN TO AVOID GETTING EATEN BY A TIGER' – they merely reinforce the legitimacy of the perceived threat, validating their anxiety, no matter how unlikely death-by-predatory-land-mammal is on the vast tundra of Hoxton Square. Exposure therapy refuses to give weight to that ancient feedback loop. It stares down the tiger and says 'AND WHAT?'

So, by staying with the anxiety and refusing to act out compulsions in the face of a 'threatening' naked Betty Boop, I'm sending a message back to my brain: 'Betty's nothing to be afraid of, neither fight nor flight will be necessary, thank you.' And because I'm doing this so often, my old lizard brain is slowly beginning to believe that it's true, meaning the myriad naked Betty Boops of the future will be less threatening.

The first time I really notice a therapeutic response working properly, I'm walking down Shoreditch High Street past a mini mall of pop-up shops – I still don't quite understand what a pop-up is, but they're literally popping up every-where – when a 149 double decker bus, bearing a huge photo of Lara Stone in a Calvin Klein bra, pulls up alongside me. I look up. Four metres of perfect womanly flesh. Four metres of perfect OCD triggers. Anxiety licks up my throat, as of old, but now it is fucking GAME TIME.

'She looks so. damn. hot' I say out loud, smiling, as I walk alongside the crawling bus, nipple height, not caring if pass-ersby hear me. 'She looks soooo freaking hot,' I say again as I stride on, taking care to really *believe* the words – they must not be rote, I must really *feel* them. And, yeah, there's anxiety, and yeah, there are doubts – *does that mean I'm gay? does that mean I'm gay? does that mean I'm gay?* – but I resist the compulsion to answer. I resist the compulsion to ruminate. I turn a corner and I resist the compulsion to look back at the bus and analyse whether or not the photo turned me on. 'Maybe,' I say out loud, 'may-fucking-be.'

And after a couple of minutes of resisting my compulsions and accepting my doubts, the funniest thing happens: I forget about the bus and the foot-long tits more quickly than I'd ever forgotten an obsession through distraction or ratio-nalisation or prayer. And when I notice this has happened I trigger afresh, of course – *maybe the fact that I'm still thinking about them means I liked them* – but *still* I do not give in. I refuse to ruminate and the thoughts fade once more.

Since the age of 15 I've tried *so* many things and held *so* many hopes, I've used so much energy and so much time, I've experienced millions of obsessions and enacted millions of compulsions, and this is the first time in my life that anything has showed the slightest sign of working. I HAVE GOT THE POWER. I am He-Man and She-Ra right now and my fists are made of lightning.

Thoughts don't exist in a vacuum called The Mind. When we think thoughts, something very physical is happening: neurons are firing off in our brains. And when we think *repetitive* thoughts, lots of neurons are firing one after another, which causes them to get wired together into neural pathways. So the more repetitive thoughts we think, the stronger these neural pathways become, and the more automatically they become the 'go to' channels for our thoughts. This is why it sometimes feels like we literally 'can't stop thinking' about something, and why anxiously ruminating only leads to more anxiety.

There is no consensus about the extent to which our thoughts can influence brain function in this way. Is there a malfunction in the brains of OCD sufferers that leads them to develop the disorder? Or is it their compulsive, self-defeating behaviour that leads their brains to malfunction? We don't know. But neuroimaging brainscans of people with OCD do show big changes before and after treatment has taught them to think differently, and the visuals are quite mesmerising. Sections of the brain, once angrily flaring, appear to glow softer, suggesting a most mind-blowing possibility: we can change our brains, *physically*. This breathtakingly beautiful phenomenon is called neuroplasticity, and for me it means that by resisting the temptation to ruminate, I'm physically rerouting my brain's neural pathways – working in the dark to undo my mind's million tiny carvings.

So the way we choose to think could, over time, change the physical structure of our bodies. Perhaps our brains are not immutable lumps to which we're yoked at birth. Perhaps they are plastic and malleable and we have the power to remould them. How exquisite. How awe-inspiring. No matter how hopeless you feel, there is always this: your brain is not static, it can change. Things can always change.

I See You Baby

When I was 16, the school took us on a religious retreat to Stratford (the birthplace of Shakespeare, not the Westfield Centre, though at that age the latter would probably have been more appealing). We stayed in some sort of holy building next to a church for the weekend. There were games and songs and lots and lots of praying.

I'd started puzzling over my Christian education many years earlier, when I'd realised that Jesus was a Jew. Curiously, no-one at my Catholic school had ever dwelled on this fact, and it'd blown my tiny mind when I'd discovered it. *Jesus was a JEW!* I remember asking a teacher in my ten-year-old's squeak why *we* weren't Jews, seeing as Jesus Christ was the best person ever and we were supposed to be Christ-like? I don't remember the answer, but I remember feeling like it wasn't good enough. Just like it wasn't good enough that dogs weren't allowed in heaven – I'd decided that any God who excluded dogs and hamsters from the hereafter was not my sort of person. More disillusionment followed when I was being taught the anti-materialistic parables of St. Luke's Gospel at the same time that my parish church was receiving a costly makeover of plushest red and gold.

By the time I went on retreat my atheism was already taking root, but I wagered, à la Pascal, that praying to God to take away my near-constant paedophilic thoughts was still worth a shot. I'd even developed religious rituals – a really common OCD compulsion. I had a strict regimen of reading three bible passages a night and saying three prayers: the Hail Mary, the Our Father and the Mea Culpa. I had to do this before I went to sleep to bring a sense of completeness to my day's attempts at expunging my doubts.

As a kid I'd once heard a Texan woman on TV say that whenever she had a problem she 'kissed it up to God' and it made her problems go away. I'd watched as she put her hands into the praying position and kissed them, then raised them to the ceiling like she was releasing a dove. So on retreat I lay there on my bunk in the dark kissing my 'sinful' thoughts up to God as I did every night now, in the hope he'd take them away.

But in the morning I woke up the same, as I did every morning, and when the bell rang for breakfast I sat around the table and laughed and joked with my friends to belie my secrets.

A big part of fitting in on retreat was looking good, because more and more people were getting cameras, and we all knew that before too long, after those little plastic dustbins had been to Happy Snaps and back, glossy piles of photos would be handed round the common room and analysed in excruciating teenage detail.

When the day came we all leaned into little huddles to see if we were winners. There was one picture of me that I liked – the sunlight was soft on my angles and I was wearing my absolute favourite Groove Armada T-shirt: 'I SEE YOU BABY' on the front; 'SHAKIN' THAT ASS' on the back. The

Black Country was still pre-digital in those days, and seeing my peers look at a flattering photo of me was thrilling in a novel way – kind of intoxicating. But in the same set there was a photo which gave me double chins I never knew I had and made my spots look a right mess, and seeing my peers look at it was *painful* in a novel way. I was suddenly aware of my appearance as I'd never been before.

When Facebook came into our lives a few years later, I remember being relieved that it hadn't been around when I was at school. I remember thinking how savage I'd have found it if I could have repeatedly gone back to the good photo and the bad photo, building up my shaky self esteem with one and slashing it with the other. I'd have checked and rechecked those images, again and again, I'm sure. I'd have recreated them in the mirror, trying to pin down what I did right and what I did wrong, trying to figure out which was the truer representation of my appearance, compulsively searching for satisfactory answers to unanswerable questions.

Digital technology is growing so fast that 'digital technology' is probably already a massively uncool thing to say. And the truism that it's growing fast is probably even less cool. But I think it's beautiful nonetheless. It gives voice to the voiceless and connects people who might otherwise be friendless or alone or uneducated. And it's awe-inspiring to see small collectives taking down grandfatherly institutions on Twitter, and kids wowing the world with their wisdom on YouTube, and all sorts of freaks and geeks uploading their funny, silly, stupid shit – shit that they make for the sheer joy of it.

But my personal relationship with it has always been kind of complicated, because, like many obsessives, I always used it self-defeatingly. I used to spend hours selecting the MySpace profile song which most perfectly conveyed who I wanted people to think I was. I used to recheck recently-uploaded status updates 15 times an hour – *why does no-one Like me?* I used to take self-portraits of myself specifically for purpose of analysing how I looked. There was no doubt about it: I was compulsively drawn to the affirmation that an image-centric online world could offer me, and it never did me much good. So now, like the mouse deer who is drawn to the irresistible stink of the dangerous-tasty durian fruit, I approach its spiny husk with caution.

I knew my online reassurance-seeking had gone too far when I found myself in Havana, Cuba, in 2013, with no camera charger and no hope of buying a replacement. Discovering that the cable wasn't in my bag was like finding out that a distant relative had died – the sense of loss was palpable. It was absurd and ugly and I didn't admit it to myself at the time, but I'm pretty sure I was mourning all the Likes I wouldn't get – all the validation that my holiday would never receive.

I chose Cuba because people said it was about to disappear. Capitalism was taking root, the old buildings were falling down, and the vintage cars would soon be gone forever. There was an urgent energy on the streets there – the creaks of a bow about to break in high wind. Art deco sports stadiums, crumbling in the Caribbean heat. Baroque porticos, covered in ferns. Blink and you'll miss it all, people said.

By day three of my holiday I was surprised that the sense of disappointment was waning, and I felt lighter for being camera-less and miles from WiFi. One afternoon I river-trekked in a national park just outside Trinidad, stopping at a waterfall shaded by corojo palms, to swim—

A flicker in the hibiscus. I gasped. A hummingbird had come to feed, two metres from where I was stood – a dazzle of iridescent blue against the flowers' carmine pink, a haze of little wings beating all about the brilliant shimmering body, a giant little bee. I could feel the buzz in my chest.

He'd be alive forever in a little electronic folder named Cuba if I'd had my camera that day. He'd be mine to admire whenever I pleased. But as time passes it seems less of a shame that he is not. Because when unbidden thoughts have perverted your life's every moment, when your mind has taken you away from yourself a million tiny times, with obsessive buzzes and alerts you loathed yet could not resist, you begin to crave the simple, unfettered rawness of seeing and hearing with your body and nothing more.

The corojo palm flickered in a brisk breeze and the bird darted and was gone. Twenty breathless seconds was all it had been. No promise of the hereafter, nothing to keep – just the urgent flutter of now.

Suck It Up

After my epiphany with Bus Tits on Shoreditch High Street, I soon realise that old habits die hard. Like a true obsessive I cling to the newfound relief of therapy too fiercely, and I start to obsess about what the *absence* of anxiety might mean. My therapist is unsurprised by this new development.

'It's not unusual for clients to become anxious about *not* being anxious,' she says, 'especially when they start to see improvements in their condition.'

She goes on to explain that the presence of anxiety had been a kind of paradoxical reassurance for me, like it'd offered some kind of proof that I was unwell, and not experiencing a real life identity crisis. Now, the *absence* of that proof has become a whole new obsession: if I'm not anxious about the thought of getting off with a woman, maybe I'm comfortable with, even desirous of, the idea.

'And you know what, Rose?'

'What?'

'You just gotta suck it up. You gotta accept that doubt. Maybe you're less anxious now because you're finally realising that – yeah – maybe you're gay. And you'll never know whether or not that's true.'

Inside your head you have 100 billion neurons, and each of these is connected to 10,000 other neurons. That makes a mini universe, buzzing with a quadrillion synapses. The brain is a phenomenal thing and beneath the rough waves every person with OCD knows this. Sometimes, when the anxiety isn't too bad, you can feel your brain working inside your head – if you watch it very carefully you can see its flits and tumbles, the hare darting between the thickets.

Once you've learned to watch, you can enter the atto-second and therein be dazzled by the brain's million contra-dictions, learnings and reroutings. Notice your thoughts at precisely the right moment – just before some deep synaptic shudder – and you can feel the lurch as the old ball bearings begin to trundle once more.

Thoughts can make you trigger, but so can a lack of thoughts. A noxious mental image will spark obsessions, but if your brain has a rare obsession-free moment, you can feel it scan itself like a searchlight for something to chew on, and as soon as you're aware of its search – boom – it finds some-thing: a memory of an older thought, usually.

Unhappiness can make you trigger, but so can happiness. An unhappy day can be used by your brain as evidence that your obsession is true, but so can happiness. In my experi-ence the very act of laughing can trigger an instantaneous obsessive question: am I really happy?

Years later I will objectively marvel at this mind-trickery. I will wonder at OCD's Machiavellian brilliance as it allows us, in the same heartbeat, to hold two paradoxical thoughts. First: maybe I'm *not anxious* because I know I'm gay, prompting anxiety. Second: maybe I'm *anxious* because I know I'm gay.

But right now I'm done with tricks. I'm exhausted. Some-times when I've had a particularly obsessive day I feel like

I'm back at the start, just as bad as I've always been, even though we're months and months into therapy.

Every week my therapist starts by asking me how I've been feeling, and every week I tell her that x, y, z, has happened and I'm *still* not completely better. I tell her that no matter how much I try to embrace ambiguity, go against my every inclination, screw up my fists and really *believe* that the last ten years of my life might have been an elaborate cover up for my latent homosexuality, the doubts are still there. They. Won't. Go. Away. Every week I tell her that I can't go on until I get rid of this doubt from my life.

'But if you can't accept doubt, Rose, you won't *have* much of a life,' she tells me on several occasions.

But one day it really gets me.

'I will. I need it,' I snap at her. 'I should have a life like everyone else.' I turn off the video on the call. 'I'm tired of feeling like everyone else in the world is part of some massive secret that I'm not a part of. I'm tired of not even being able to have a therapy session without even my *therapist* getting all twisted into sex in my head. It's bullshit—'

'I know, Rose . . .' She leaves it open for me to speak but I don't say anything. 'I can't see you in the video, maybe we've lost connection.'

I click the screen and peep beyond my clutched knees at the little square of me in the bottom right corner of the screen.

'Rose, listen to me. I know it's been hard, this therapy *is* hard. But, you know, no-one's life is free from doubt. That's an illusion, and if that's what you're aiming for then you know you're setting yourself up for a struggle with reality, aren't you?'

'Yes.'

'All these things we talk about every week like imperfection, ambiguity, uncertainty, *unhappiness*, even – they're all part of everyone's life. You think getting better is synonymous with banishing those things, but it's not, you've got to learn to accept them.'

'Okay,' I mumble from behind my hair.

'I really think "getting better" has now become a fixation in itself for you, Rose. I see it all the time. It's just another form of compulsive behaviour. And as we know, compulsions make obsessions worse. The slightest shred of anxiety threatens how you think things should be, and what you think your identity should be. And I'm tellin' you now, if want to get better, you have to accept that anxiety might *always* be a part of your life, and that you might never get completely better. It might *never* be perfect. And that's how we live, all of us, all the time, that's the only way we're able to live.'

I pick at my cuticles. She tells me I'm doing great work, and then winds up the call because it's time, but after she's gone I don't get up. I sit still, thinking about therapy and about everything. *Compulsions make obsessions worse. Compulsions make obsessions worse. Compulsions make obsessions worse.*

I realise, now, just how much of my life has been compulsive. My refusal to tolerate anxiety. My attempt to banish OCD absolutely. My constant need for confirmation that I was unwell. My insistence on perfection with Toby. My constant need for external validation of my physical appearance. That *whole trip* around the world – it was all a futile, compulsive effort to obliterate doubt. What about listening to my loop tapes? Or my detailed manifesto for New Rose? I lie back on my bed with my legs and arms outstretched. I am stunned into stillness by the sudden unfettered realisation that I've been making myself worse my whole life, and that therapists have been, too.

I see now how striving for certainty had only made me less certain, how it'd all been so acutely self-defeating. How searching for 'Me' had only ever made me more confused. I see our constant cycle of trying to block out the scary and unknown, only to render ourselves more frightened and more insecure. If we can't tolerate discomfort, if we can't accept that others might think we're ugly or uncool or untalented, if we can't let our doubts just *be*, we sabotage ourselves.

I see now how sinister is the myth I'd believed for so long that 'positive thinking' makes positive things happen. No. It only ever made us more fearful of the Negative, only ever made us tighten our compulsive grip on a reality that's not ours to wield. And it only ever propagated the even more heartbreaking myth that if someone fails – romantically, professionally, mentally – they could have prevented it if only they'd visualised a positive alternative, if only they'd thought themselves into a positive frame of mind, if only they'd snapped out of it.

I think again of Charlene, and how, as a teenage girl, I'd swooned for her lyrics as I sat at my bedroom window, watching the Black Country sky: 'I've been to paradise but I've never been to me.' I was ready to go there. I was ready for adventure. I think again of 'The Vale Of Soul Making' – how I'd filled my young head with romance, how I'd wanted to forge a 'pure identity', like there was some elixir to being that I didn't yet know. How I'd looked forward to the great, inevitable 'falling into place' of being a grown-up. Back then I'd thought that Coming Of Age meant discovering who you are. Maybe it's more about accepting that you might never know.

In this new moment things seem clear and enormous. For the second time my life is rewritten and its million twists make sense in a new way. In the soft-light space between waking and exhausted sleep I am awed by a simple and inescapable paradox: running from your thoughts will only quicken their pace.

Dirty Little Secret

It's been a year since I started therapy and life is good. I am not cured absolutely and I no longer seek to be. Sometimes I still get knocked sideways by an obsessive doubt or mental image and it takes me hours to recover. But now I feel 'normal'. And I don't mean what I used to mean when I said that word – perfect, worry-free, breezy – I mean fucked-up in a manageable way, and it's lovely.

Nothing is concluded. Things are still expanding. I remain a curious cosmonaut through my own tiny mind, discovering new neurotic phenomena as the months roll on. The latest development seems to be a mild phonic tic, whereby I occasionally make involuntary sounds – squeaks, yelps and vocal rhythms – in response to unpleasant thoughts. It only seems to happen when I'm stressed or hyper or over-excited with too much work. As my career progresses and I'm called upon more and more to express my ideas and opinions to bigger and bigger cheeses, I find myself more and more doubtful of my abilities. And if I'm alone at the end of a frantic day, recalling an awkwardly worded sentence in a meeting or a clumsy social encounter or the sceptical glance of a friend, I feel tension building in my body until I involuntary yip, squeal or even sing out loud, releasing the tension.

I've also felt my obsessions try to shift to a new, distinctly unsexy theme: the structural integrity of buildings. Instead of dicks and minges (mingae?) I have obsessions about wooden floors caving in, Victorian chimneys collapsing in high winds, skyscrapers toppling like sawn trees. Thematically this kind of *does* make sense in the context of my previous X-rated obsessions, because the same threatening doubt is at play: something *might* happen to change everything I hold dear. Might might might. OCD is all about the mights.

But thanks to the skills that therapy has taught me, I've been able to nip this new obsession in the bud. Now, if I'm lying in bed and I have an intrusive thought about the house falling down and altering my world irrecoverably, I simply remind myself that nothing is certain. The bricks might perish. The foundations might falter. At any minute the roof might blow off. That's life.

Now I feel saner, I decide to get my story down on paper. I don't do it for any noble reason. I do it because I've always wanted to write a book and because my wants have been obscured by my condition for so long. And because I think the slow act of building something, badly, laboriously, frustratingly, word after word, is valuable. Obsessive compulsive disorder has taught me that. I spent tens of thousands of hours training my brain to obsess, and countless more thousands training it *not* to obsess – lots of tiny little moments built on top of each other, painstakingly, over years and years. The tectonic power of the human mind is awe-inspiring, and now I use it in other areas of my life which would benefit from a bit of training – French language and bass-playing and writing – because one day in a decade or two I might look back and see how the plates have shifted.

I pitch the book idea to several well-known literary agents and I get rejected by every one. Toby hugs me as I sob at the standard rejection letters: '. . . it's not quite right for our agency'; 'Though your novel was very interesting to us . . .'

'It's not even a *novel*,' I winge into Toby's wet neck, holding the wet letters in my hands. 'They don't even care.'

Toby pleads with me to stay objective and not take the responses personally. 'OH, I AM BEING OBJECTIVE,' I reply, writhing face down on the rug, the long pile sticking to my dribble-smeared face. *Oh*, I understand the moral of the exercise *perfectly*: these letters are targeted messages from the publishing industry to *me*, and they say, 'your life story is boring, your writing is pitiful, there is nothing to be learned from your experience, and you might want to consider just GROWING THE FUCK UP.'

'Oh, I understand this, Toby. I understand it LOUD. AND. CLEAR.'

But when I unfurl from the foetal position an hour later, I get real, and that week I send my book proposal to a friend who works in publishing. Happily, he seems to think that the *Guardian* might be interested in all the dicks and fannies, and tells a *Weekend* editor about them over lunch. Soon I'm drafting a 3000-word memoir feature about my life with OCD, which will run in a few weeks' time, with my giant 'I'm-thinking-about-dicks-and-fannies' face slapped on the front cover.

This is it: my coming out.

As I'm writing the article I'm aflame. I walk in a different way. I stride the streets listening to euphoric house on my headphones and fist-pumping over such minor fortuities as on-time trains and not-treading-in-dog-shit. Incredibly, I don't even grimace when children stare at me on the bus. Because someone *cares* about what I have to say.

There's lots of back and forth with the brilliant *Guardian* folk in the run up to the article, and a photographer comes to my house to take my picture. But the whole thing doesn't hit me until the morning of publication – Saturday 31st August, 2013 – when I go into Costcutter with Jack. I asked him to stay over last night because Toby's away working and I didn't want to be alone.

As soon as we walk in I see a sliver of my face peeping from the paper in a stranger's hands. And then I hear the beep as the guy behind the till scans the barcode. *Oh, God, what if the till guy reads it? Every time he serves me my groceries and fags I'm going to be thinking that he's thinking about what I'm thinking.*

I hold Jack close at my side as I inch over to the stack of Saturday papers in the corner of the shop. I dither by the tinned beans, feeling wibbly.

'Oh shit. Oh shit. Oh shit,' I say, half laughing.

'Y'am alright, bab,' Jack says in a comforting, Black Country drawl, patting me on the shoulder with a smirk. He picks up the top paper and lets it flop open heavily. There it is – my giant face on the *Weekend* cover, half a foot's worth of face, two feet of face, *miles and miles* of face.

'Oh shit.'

Jack reads the headline out loud – 'Dirty Little Secret. My X-Rated Mind: Living with Pure OCD' – and stifles an enormous laugh, then we're both giggling uncontrollably in the aisle next to the soaps and sanny pads, and I'm grabbing onto him and 'Oh shit'-ing profusely and pressing the cover to my chest in case anyone sees, as if doing so will stop 200,000 people picking it up today. My parents. Their friends. People I went to school with. They could all be entering 'my X-rated mind' as they chow down on their Marm-on-toast. Through the giggles I feel the colour drain from my face.

We buy a couple of copies each and I dizzy back home on Jack's arm, feeling peculiarly giddy, and very, very vulnerable. Several times in the two minute journey we redouble into laughter. 'Dirty. Little. Secret,' we repeat, creasing.

'Bless the fucking *Guardian*,' I say, shaking my head through the giggles. 'Butter wouldn't melt, I swear.'

The trembling begins when we get back to the flat and Jack rips open the cellophane and starts reading in silence – a story I've never told him, despite knowing him forever. I watch his face, hoping to glean some initial feedback from his expressions, but the silence and the stillness continues. He takes approximately ONE THOUSAND HOURS and I put the kettle on for some noise. When he finally puts down the paper he hugs me and tells me he's 'well proud'.

I 'phew' and pour the tea.

Now it's 8.30am and I haven't heard from anyone else. *What's everyone thinking?* Jack had somewhere to be and he's left already, and I'm on my own, sitting on the sofa, worrying. I picture the girls reading the *Guardian*'s editorial lines: 'you mentally undress your friends; you see everyone naked'. Sure enough they sum up the thrust of the article, but they seem so stark when paraphrased into sound bites. Will the girls be wincing? *Will they feel violated?* Will they think back to all the nights out we shared in Leeds and wonder if I was perving on them? It's too, too cringe.

And the public. I'm going to get savaged by the commenters online. Trolled to absolute shit. They're going to call me a paedo and a pervert and a closet case and a homophobe—

And then the calls start coming and they don't stop for hours. Toby and Patty and Ted and Maggie and the girls. No judgment. No embarrassment. No resentment at all the duplicity. Everyone is crying and saying they love me, and I am crying and saying I love them back, and I have never felt more loved or more alive.

But now it's 10.30am and I still haven't heard from my parents. Are they just too bewildered by all porn talk to get in touch? I've anticipated their handling of this news all my life, and having tried and failed to tell them that time a couple of years ago – after Toby found the cuts – I can't believe I've finally let it all out.

I always imagined I'd do it in a much more passive way. Perhaps sending them a link or asking them to Google 'OCD with sexual doubts' or something, getting them to do the research so I didn't have to articulate it. I'd imagined the scene in precise detail. Dad sitting at the yellowing PC and typing the letters on the creaky keys, one by one, with his two outstretched index fingers:

OCd THERAPY\

I imagined him looking up at the flickering screen, scrunching his nose to reselect the cursor, and with slow, methodical mouse-work clicking <u>Treatment</u> with two precise and determined taps. He'd have started reading, had to stop a few times, perhaps, before getting to the end. He'd have printed out the pages and left them on Mom's pillow for her to find. Then, next morning as he watched the bird feeder from the window and scraped the blackened toast crumbs into the bin, scraping long after the black had gone, all Mom would've kept saying to him would've been, 'It must be so exhausting, so exhausting.'

I imagined them thinking about the exposure, not understanding and feeling helpless, like they felt when I used to bring maths home from school with whines. I imagined them thinking about the porn. Their little girl watching porn, for *therapy* – times have really changed.

I imagined the first time they saw me after I broke the news. I imagined them trying to take my mind off things by asking about my job, about what's happening with Toby now, about the neighbour's guttering project and how the dog at Dad's fishing club keeps getting into the cowfield. I imagined them wondering if I'm really here or if I'm off somewhere battling some unspeakable thought. I imagined Dad's hand on Mom's hand – a fast bind of wedding-banded flesh, and their two sets of eyes, worried, the lines cross-hatching the delicate skin between their brows—

The phone rings. It's Mom. Two rings. Three rings. Four rings. I gulp and answer.

'Hello?'

'Hello *bibiche*.' She sounds winded.

'Hi Mom.' There is a pause. I can't think of anything to say.

'Well, *Boubou*—' she starts, faltering, 'your dad and I have read your article and well—you were right—it really was a shock.'

'I know—'

'We just—*don't know* how you coped. We don't know. We don't know. And we're so sorry that you had to go through that all *rubbish* on your own,' she almost loses her voice. 'But all we can do is thank God, *thank God*, that you're okay.'

'I am okay, I promise.'

'Oh, *biche*, I'm *so*, so glad.' Another pause. 'We love you and we're so, so very proud of you.'

'Thank you, *Maman*. I love you.'

We hang up. 'I love you, Mom,' I say again, out loud, to no-one.

That's it, I think, *my secret's out*. A lifetime of performance, of acting as happy as I thought I was supposed to feel, and now this, a disillusion, a relinquishing of false self.

'Here I am,' I whisper.

I look down at the hands which grasp the phone. For the first time in over a decade the skin on my thumbs is smooth and not-bleeding and unbroken.

Beep. A tweet from a stranger: 'Thank god I'm not alone.' Then another: 'I've waited 40 years to read something like that.' Then an email from a teenage girl: 'You may have just changed my life.' And they keep coming so fast I can't count them. I pore over them in tears, feeling connected for the first time to the millions of strangers out there who understand. I think of my own epiphany in my uni room all those years ago, when I first discovered that I wasn't alone – that there were people out there who were just like me. And now these people are speaking to me. All different ages from all over the world, and we are all not-alone together.

Then one little email knocks the breath from my chest. It's from a 52-year-old woman who, like me, had been a student at Leeds University and had kept her OCD secret most of her life. It reads: 'I showed my mother your article as I knew that, although she might find it painful, she would want to know. I have often said to her that I felt that no-one else shared my pain. She cried when she read it. I put my arms around her and told her she wasn't to blame and that I'd just been born in the wrong time, in a time when no-one understood these things. I think that time is about to change.'

Other Buttock Injuries

Eleven years. Eleven years. Eleven years.

It was eleven years from the night I first experienced obsessive compulsive disorder to the day I found the therapy which saved my life. Sometimes even now my knees falter at the memory of the climb, at how many nights I spent bleating on the slopes. How did this happen to me? Why is it still happening to people today? Why does it typically take obsessives between eight and twelve *years* to access effective therapy? How have I, and millions like me, been so spectacularly let down by the professionals charged with our care? I am sitting here with my medical records and a large glass of white, trying to find out.

But again and again, reading these intimate pages written by strangers – a diary I don't remember writing – I am distracted by a thousand emotions. So many times over the years the body darts down doctors' corridors, hiding from the harrying swoop of mortality, and when these warrened years are seen all at once from above, like this, what you get is a vast, daft tangle of indignity.

In 1988 when I was two years old, a doctor scribbled 'Infection right buttock' under 'Other Buttock Injuries'. No more details. In 91, a bedwetting update: 'Dry at day. Never at night. Using nappies.' To 96 and my *triumphant* first year of double figures: 'I saw Rose a week or so ago with vaginal discharge, there seemed to be no obvious cause for this except perhaps she was wiping her bottom the wrong way' (an accusation I most *strenuously* deny). Moving on to the digital age, February 2003, when anonymous Times New Roman sums up my teenage joie-de-vivre with alarming accuracy: 'Avoids even the most trivial exercise', and the following year, when I succumbed to the archdemon: 'Acne vulgaris'.

Vulgaris. Vulgar. Common. What strikes me reading this pimpled history is how secret it is, and how uncommonly we're exposed to real vulgarity. The ladies in the papers, sucked in and sexualised and so terribly unvulgar and unnaked, are fully exposed yet reveal so little; the teenagers with their affected gaits and Facebook-faces, all belying the glorious-gooey reality of women and girls, which must remain whispered to doctors in the warrens. Maybe that's why spots are so repugnant to our sensibilities – because in their puffy red-and-yellowness they put the inside out, they spill the beans.

Then the tenderness comes, to read long-forgotten snippets of my childhood. 'Rose's mother insists there was infection present'. Yes, I hear her voice here – she always insists most passionately where her children are concerned. 'Rose was brought to hospital' tells the story of Mom or Dad holding me in a waiting room. Were they worried? Did we have to wait long? (Maybe I'd pulled some attention-seeking fake illness trick – a tendency of which I was once so ashamed, but for which I can now forgive myself – it was mental illness, it was not my fault.) And the sweetness of the doctors who called me 'little girl' and 'little one' and 'little lass'. So strange to hear my big body referred to like this. Stranger, still, to read a line, typed in Courier, under the heading

'Follow Up Appointments': '5th January 2061 – Elderly Heath Assessment.'

The rage comes when I go deeper, armed with a highlighter and Post-It notes. In fluorescent pink I mark the first reference to my mental health, where someone's typed 'depressed' – the willy dance doctor who'd wanted my improvement as a percentage – must've been. Following this is a cluster of psychiatrists' letters. I recognise the names of various medical buildings and roads in Leeds – terraces and crescents and rows with shiny cobbles and gurgling drains and drippy trees – which I'd forgotten, but which I now remember with awesome story-time chills. These letters record a rambling set of assessments and appointments with various doctors spanning many months.

Reading these letters, which make no mention of OCD, I wonder whether the lack of diagnosis was my fault – maybe I generalised my symptoms because as a teenager I was too embarrassed to articulate the specifics of my doubts? If I was sugar-coating the uncomfortable truth then it's no wonder the professionals couldn't get to the bottom of what was wrong with me. But I 'oh' audibly, sadly, to see that I gave a near-textbook definition of OCD as early as February 2005, some seven years before I accessed effective treatment:

'Rose told me that she has been suffering from anxiety symptoms and low mood since the age of 15 years. During that time she had very distressing ruminations about children experiencing abuse and mental images of this. Though she herself has not experienced any abuse, she found these thoughts and images extremely uncomfortable ... Rose seems to be currently suffering from a mixed anxiety and depressive episode.'

I feel my face getting hot now, and notice that I'm screwing my fist into a feeble ball around the highlighter. *Depressive episode? Why wasn't OCD diagnosed here?* The question feels pathetic and my anger feels pathetic. For a few seconds I fantasise about stepping back in time and switching the tracks just half an inch to change the course of the rest of my life. But I've learnt that fixating on unchangeable things is fruitless, and I move on.

Another appointment and another letter, where for the first time in all this I hear my frustrations straining through the psychiatrist's words, trying to articulate what's really wrong:

'We spent time today discussing how Rose feels that her main problem rather than being depression or anxiety is actually that she experiences a lot of intrusive thoughts and images. This started at about the age of 15 when she started imagining small children in different sexual positions and had constant images come to her mind about this which cause much distress. She says this causes her to constantly ask herself questions about why she is experiencing these thoughts and makes herself feel extremely guilty. She is particularly upset when she has intrusive thoughts about women and worries that she may be gay though she doesn't think that this is the case. Rose tries to deal with these thoughts by distracting herself, for example, watching television, or she tries to engage with them and find out why they don't make sense, but neither approach helps. I spent time today normalising intrusive thoughts and images with Rose and I have given her a list of bizarre thoughts and images experienced by a non-clinical sample of people.'

Then the tears come. I swipe a fluro box around the

paragraph. '"Normalising intrusive thoughts?"' I say out loud, 'Fuck that.' I take a swig of wine. All this doctor had done was collude in my self-defeating behaviour, as if I hadn't already tried a *million* times to remind myself that ambiguous thoughts were normal. She'd essentially been acting out a compulsion for me, giving an alcoholic a drink. She'd made me less anxious in the moment, I'm sure – I actually remember the sense of clarity that such affirmations from doctors gave me – but in doing so she'd facilitated my futile, lifelong compulsive need to avoid ambiguity at all costs. I look down. The page is pulping where the nib has bled. My nails have made little indentations in my palm.

I read on. It's not until after I'd diagnosed myself and I was well into that 20-week course of psychodynamic therapy, that I see OCD mentioned for the first time. The clinical psychologist writes:

'Rose attended well and began to make connections from her past to her current functioning in the present . . . When Rose experienced normal sexual feelings and thoughts, she did not understand them and thought they were shameful and that something was wrong with her. However, the more the she tried not to think sexual things the worse the imagery became making her feel worse about herself. Part of Rose wanted a diagnosis (such as OCD). This validated her feelings and allowed her to be unwell (a bit like when she was a child) although Rose is much more aware of the dangers of staying in the sick role.'

I spray a mist of Chenin on the page and bark one black laugh before wibbling into an open mouthed sob. 'Making connections between my thoughts and my past?' *I mean, fuck*! Isn't that what I've been trying to do myself all these years: compulsively wringing my childhood for any memory which might hint at my sexual identity? *Again. Again. Again*: A therapist encouraging compulsive behaviour, this time by attributing meaning to intrusive thoughts, as if I could somehow *think* them out of my head by unlocking my subconscious. My subconscious! I'd been dredging that nebula for clues myself for years, and it'd only ever kept the vicious cycle spinning.

I once heard OCD specialist Dr David Veale say that 'therapists love complexity, which is why they don't like the "B" in cognitive behavioural therapy, because it doesn't look at reasons *why* we're depressed. They love to ask 'why' rather than 'how', even though that amounts to rumination.' Now I see that toxic fixation on 'why' in these records – all these therapists who wanted to root around in my past for whys. Exposure therapy works so well because it isn't bothered about 'why', it focuses on the 'how' of behaviour, in the moment – teaching you *how* to behave when you're exposed to triggers, teaching you not to deepen the grooves through rumination.

I read the letter again. 'The sick role.' Even now this makes me anxious. I'm better but not all-better, after all. *Maybe I DID make the whole thing up for attention?* I'd faked illness when I was a kid, who's to say I'm not doing it now? It's here in writing. This doctor had psychoanalysed me and concluded that OCD is a role I play to hide latent truths.

I pour myself another glass and shrug. *I'll never know for certain if that's true.*

And that's where the history of my mental health trails off, because I wrote the rest of it myself with private therapy: the New Rose therapy followed by the intensive therapy – floppy failures the lot. So why did I keep going back? Why did I physically take myself to those places every week?

It's difficult to overestimate how powerful the influence of a therapist can be. I once met a girl who'd been paying for a private therapist for years. The therapist had been repeatedly reassuring her that her obsessive violent thoughts did not reflect intent. He'd even offered in-the-moment reassurance via telephone when she was panicking – always encouraging her to rationalise her OCD doubts. As a result she'd developed a compulsive dependence on the fleeting (and expensive) relief his reassurances offered.

And because so many clinicians collude in dangerous relief-seeking behaviour, many patients will vehemently defend even the most inept therapist, as they don't want their source of comfort being jeopardised. In the same way that a drug addict will find a thousand reasons to justify their next fix, many OCD patients will find reasons why their chosen therapist is the best one for them. During the New Rose therapy I really, really wanted to believe that it was working, and ironically the therapy's doomed central tenet – that if I thought positive things, positive feelings would follow – was what kept me believing.

And it's all so terribly unnecessary. Because the right kind of therapy *can* completely cure obsessive compulsive disorder. I once met a man whose untreated paedophilia obsession had been so compelling, he'd confessed to his wife that he thought he'd sexually abused their kids. The police had taken him away and he'd spent a night in the cells before a shrink had diagnosed him. It nearly cost him his marriage – the horror is unfathomable. Now, mercifully, he is post-treatment and completely free of OCD.

I stare at the last page of my medical records and lean my head back against the sofa arm. As my body sinks down I loosen my grip on the paper and the sheets slide from my fingers and fan across the floor like the petals of a shattered bouquet.

Tingling, heaviness, haze: body emotions.

Bewildered, I can pluck only one phrase from the ether: What the fuck? It repeats itself in my mind: *What the fuck? What the fuck? What the fuck?* and then I realise I'm saying it out loud. I'm standing up and crying it or laughing it, I don't know: 'WHAT THE FUCK?' How is it okay that this is happening? How is it okay that hundreds of thousands of people with a very treatable condition cannot be taught the simple skills they need to manage their lives? Why is access to good NHS therapy dependent on a postcode lottery? Why are waiting lists so long that they're pushing people into private therapy, which is often piss-poor and bank-breakingly expensive? Still standing, I start scribbling on a bit of paper, scratching out sums and subtractions until I reach a total:

10,000. I've spent *ten grand* on private therapists.

None of it makes sense.

Obsessives are running riot, I swear. Log in to any online OCD 'help' forum and you'll hear them screaming as if from under ice, doling out well-meaning but disastrous advice to other obsessives. And it's no wonder – understanding OCD is an ongoing process among clinicians who've trained for decades, let alone among lay teenagers in their bedrooms. While OCD was classed as an anxiety disorder in 1994 by the Diagnostic and Statistical Manual of Mental Disorders, a revised edition in 2015 recategorised the condition as a separate disorder: 'OCD and Related Disorders'. This revision reflects the observation that anxiety is not always the driving force behind the problem, and that other aversive states such as disgust, guilt, shame and physical and psychological discomfort, may dominate the internal experience. There's not even a consensus about whether or not it's a mental 'illness'. Some obsessives and clinicians find the definition helpful in that it generates empathy, decreases the likelihood of blame, and authenticates the OCD experience. Others think this medicalisation of the disorder creates unnecessary 'excess baggage' for such a common neurotic experience.

But never mind definitions, how have we not even got the *name* figured out yet? 'Pure O' is used by many sufferers to differentiate themselves from the much more publicised obsessive compulsive cleaners, and it's culturally valuable for that reason – we simply didn't *exist* in public consciousness until this term gave us a way of describing our invisible experiences. But 'pure O' is a confusing misnomer, because by definition OCD can never be 'purely obsessional'. The compulsions, though often subtle or mental, are very much there, and respond to the same treatment used for any other 'kind' of OCD. Indeed, there are no 'kinds' of the disorder at all. There is no 'other OCD'. There is simply OCD. Regardless of the themes of the obsessions or the visibility of the compulsions, the same cyclical relationship between obsessions and compulsions remains, and the confusion over language is testament to how poorly understood, badly treated and irresponsibly reported the condition really is. The Wikipedia article about 'pure O' has recently changed its name from Purely Obsessional OCD to Primarily Obsessional OCD, also listing the possible alternatives: OCD without overt compulsions; OCD with covert compulsions; Pure-O; pure O. When Jay Z dropped his hyphen, he got a freaking press release. Where's *ours*?

It's like a teenage house party in there and it's got waaaaay out of hand. It's well beyond the tipsy, I'm-the-king-of-the-world stage. It's at the woozy, shit-just-got-dark stage, when it's 5am and there's puke seeping under the lino and bodies in granny's bed, and someone's grossly overfed the fish so that you can't see through the water anymore. WHERE ARE THE ADULTS? We need an OCD dad.

OCD Dad needs to sit everyone down cross-legged on the carpet with an orange squash and a custard cream, and impart the golden rule of OCD – the essential wisdom of which almost every sufferer stays tragically ignorant for years: COMPULSIONS MAKE OBSESSIONS WORSE. Don't be fooled, he needs to say, compulsions might make you feel better for a little while, but in the long run they just make the doubt seem bigger. The more you tussle with a thought, he needs to explain, the more likely it is to come back. And then he needs to tell us all the things we can do, and all the people who can help us do it, and show us how to find the goodies and avoid the baddies. And when he's done, we'll be all wind-swept and wibbly and we'll feel like we've been kissed on the forehead.

It's dark outside and I've got the light on in here and I catch sight of my reflection in the window. My mouth is open and I've got one hand on my chest and the other clenched by my side. I can't believe it, *any* of it. I wanna tell Oprah about it. I wanna tell Letterman about it. 'Can you *believe* it, Dave?' I'll say, and he won't be able to. I want a UN conference. I want Live Aid. I want mental health to be on the lips of every newsreader in the world. I want to talk about 3000 suicides every day, and exorcisms-as-cures, and cuts to mental health funding, and one in four people who are men-tally ill, who are not dangerous and are not freaks, and who desperately need all the resources and understanding and love in the world.

Eleven years. Eleven years. Eleven years. When I was a little kid I used to have dreams about incomprehensible things, night terrors felt in my body rather than seen in my mind: of dark, indefinable masses so big you couldn't see their edges; of great numbers – the terrifying meaninglessness of infinite zeros. Endlessness meant death in those dreams, I'm sure, and in the endless irresolution of my eleven-year search for my self, the terror was no less.

There are four thousand days in eleven years. One hundred thousand hours.

Farm Frenzy

I'm back at my folks' house. Mom and I are propped up by pillows on her bed, wrapped in fleecy blankets. Dad is on the computer in the corner of the room, as he so often is now he's learned to use 'the email'. Patty is round, too, sprawled on the sofa downstairs with a pint of orange juice and half a foot of chocolate digestives. Outside it's windy and rainy and occasionally Mom tuts involuntarily when the wind rattles the windows. We are glad to be inside together.

I'm on my laptop and Mom's on hers. Dad had given it to her as a birthday present a couple of years ago because she likes to play card games and collect photos of the family on it. When I'd accidentally smashed *my* laptop on the floor and couldn't afford to buy a new one, she'd freely lent me hers, which had touched me because I knew how much she loved it. Doing my therapy homework, I'd felt guilty Googling all that X-rated stuff on her machine, and it pleases me to see her on it now. I'm checking Facebook and Twitter and boring myself, and she's grumbling in French at Patience, which amuses me greatly.

I encourage her to try some of the demo games installed on her laptop – with the relish of a kid egging on a friend to do something clearly inadvisable, like eating a bag of Monster Munch in a minute – just for shits and gigs. She clicks on Farm Frenzy 2 and lets out a hyperbolic 'euggggh' to see the character design – bulbous pigs and chickens with googly eyes. She scrunches up her nose as the game's panoramic farmyard opens up, and reads the on-screen text aloud: 'This is a chicken. It eats grass and produces eggs.'

'A chicken eating GRASS?' she shrieks, the Frenchest person in the world right now. 'Since *when*?' She tries to feed the chicken grass but it walks the other way.

'*Merde.*'

I'm laughing with her and at her but she doesn't mind. The generation gap entertains us both. Dad is chuckling in the corner. If the dog was still alive she'd be charging up the stairs demanding to know what the fracas was all about.

'You have to water the grass to feed your animals . . . *mais, alors.*' She stabs the mouse at the water well a few times. '—EH,' she shrieks, 'the well is *empty*? *Ce n'est pas possible.*'

Then loads of chickens start running about on the screen and she's saying '*je ne comprend pas*' over and over, and I'm belly laughing. There are tears in my eyes I'm laughing so much, and I notice how incredibly happy I am, the kind of happiness which sends sentences from unwritten letters rushing through your mind – letters you promise you'll send but probably never will. In this moment I am privileged to be one of the only people of this earth who's been in this 1950s semi, in this higgledy-piggledy bedroom above the back loo where Patty used to spit on the woodlice, listening to the tannoy from the train station muffling through the big trees.

As kids we want to bottle such moments. We want to screw the cap on with our chubby hands, really tight, and keep the feelings forever. The tales we're told of happily-ever-after get into our little minds and feed our little dreams, and the grown-ups see this. So they give us hamsters and rabbits – furry little lives scuttling towards their end – to show us that sometimes bad things happen that we cannot control. We are shell-shocked and we cry as we ceremoniously seal the shoebox, but we understand. And the next day we're out in the garden, sick with laughter, slinging cat poo onto the neighbours' roof.

Somewhere along the way, through the storm of adolescence, I lost that acceptance. I could not accept the looming unknowns of loving and being loved, and I tried to bring them within the compass of my control. But now that I'm on my way to 30 and inescapably a grown-up, I have taken my hands off the handlebars for the first time, and it's okay.

It's okay because I no longer believe the Hollywood lie that everything happens for a reason. The Hollywood lie of neatness and conclusion and The End. The Hollywood lie that if you love someone hard enough you can make them happy.

Sometimes love isn't enough, and that's okay. Sometimes you can scream your love at someone with all your strength but their expression won't change and their eyes will continue to stare at something huge and terrifying in the distance that you can't see and will never understand. Sometimes illness or bereavement or bullying can scorch a person's life so fiercely that no-one else can find their way through the smoke to the charred person inside. Happiness is never forgetting that.

Happiness is staring down the insurmountable fragility of

life and daring to acknowledge the certainty that everything which makes us who we are could, at any second, and without warning, be obliterated in the beat of a hummingbird's wing. And loving till it hurts and playing Farm Frenzy anyway.

The Very Best Of Pure R&B

Within a week of Toby and I moving in together, I totally Lennie our new flat.

It's a Friday night and the two of us are going out with our respective friends. I'm desperate to show off the new place, so I invite Jack over for a glass of wine and cheese, because that is what real adults do – real adults with proper jobs who move in with their partners.

We have a single glass, in a wine glass with a stem – because proper adults savour their wine and definitely don't drink it out of pint glasses. Then we walk to the pub down the road. As we cheers our first drinks we very sternly assert that we're only going to have two halves, on account of the fact that Jack has to be up in the morning and I've got to write when I get home. Each not quite trusting the other's capacity for bad influence, there are many earnest 'no seriouslys' on both parts.

I don't know when the failing begins, if it's when we decide not to order food because 'we'll eat when we get home', or if it's when we make our second and 'final' drink a 6.6% Leffe, or if it's when we bump into Billy, our mutual friend, and use this happy coincidence as justification for uttering the fateful phrase, 'just one more'. (Note, here, the dictionary definition of 'fateful' as 'having far-reaching and typically disastrous consequences.')

Whenever it begins, it soon leads to a fourth Leffe and toilet paper stuck to my shoe and chatting to strangers like they're brethren, then, not really knowing how, I'm back at my new flat with Billy and Jack and we're listening to *The Very Best of Pure R&B: The Summer Collection*, *very* loud, and making cocktails that are three parts vodka, one part Peanut Punch; then Toby's friend Jeff, who by chance is walking past the flat on the way back from a night out, pokes his head through the open window and I'm inviting him in along with his four mates; 'PACK EM IN' I'm bellowing down the road, arms flailing wildly; then Jack's getting cavalier with Toby's spirits collection and everyone's got a tumbler full of gin and orange squash, and there are heart-to-hearts and Frangelico shots and dancing on the sofa and Craig David—

Then my memory goes black. There's no middling haze, no sleepy giggles. Just an instant, unremarkable severance – the curtains abruptly drawn, snapping out the last sliver of the evening's dignity.

The next day, Toby fills me in about what happened next, and I writhe in oscillation between laughter and frantic remorse as he sets the scene:

He comes home at 2am to find an all but empty flat, lights still on, spilt cocktails everywhere and the place full of fag smoke; me sprawled on our bed, soaking wet and naked, with the bedroom door wide open, the bathroom soaked where I'd sat in the bottom of the shower after being sick; Jack face down on the sofa with his arms by his side, wearing his full suit and his shoes, like he'd been ritually put in a coffin the wrong way up in disgrace.

'What the fuck?' Toby says aloud, not knowing who I'd been out with, and walks up to the strange body lying in the dark in his brand new home. Jack doesn't stir when Toby checks his pulse, although he reportedly lets out a soft whinny of satisfaction when Toby lays a blanket over him.

If I'd been Toby I'd be screaming at this point, no doubt: 'WHAT THE FUCK HAPPENED?' . . . 'YOU'RE CLEAN-ING THIS UP' . . . 'YOU SMELL LIKE SHIT'. But Toby – and this I *do* remember – calmly gets ready for bed and slides between the sheets next to me, lying very close.

'You've Lennied the flat already, haven't you?' he whis-pers, stroking my hair. 'Because you loved it too much.' He kisses me on the forehead and turns out the light. And even though my mind is hammering through the exosphere and my mouth is a limestone cave, I am able to pull a thought from the darkness: somehow, against the odds, I don't know how I've done it, but I have – I've reached into the whirling billions and found the best boy in the world.

I still don't believe in 'the one'. I don't think there was anything fateful in my meeting Toby or that there's any higher force keeping us together. Not even Love is keeping us together – poor, diaphanous, airbrushed Love, which has so much responsibility on its shoulders. The only thing keeping us together is our choice to be here, every day. And amid the humming of our daily routine – the listening and the being listened to, the arguments and the silences, the beige dinners and the *King of the Hill* marathons, I am often blindsided by serendipitous blooms of irrational, silly love, which cannot be sought or controlled or willed into being. And if it wasn't for the comparative cacophony of OCD,

I now wonder, would these moments feel so impossibly beautiful in their sheer, simple unthinkingness?

I broke the sofa that night, too – at some point during the forgotten hours, I guess – and I can feel the snapped wood underneath me now as I lie here with Toby, a year later.

He's lying in front of me and I'm stroking his short hair against the grain with the bristly brush. Whenever I stop he tilts his head back and roots against my hand, because he can never get enough of the bristly brush. Even if he's trying to be serious about something he'll stop midsentence, mid-*word*, and smile, if he feels the brush against the back of his head.

We're watching *Lost in Translation* and I am absorbed by the twinkling city lights which float, bright and soft, across the screen, flaring in reds and yellows and blues and pinks, immersing me and taking me to Tokyo.

When the strip club scene comes on and a naked girl spins across the screen, I feel Toby's body tense up in my arms as he holds his breath – he is afraid for me because he knows the OCD thoughts still come sometimes.

I shuffle on the sofa as an obsessive doubt swells up from the back of my mind – *maybe I'd be happier in a relationship with a girl* – bringing me back inside of myself with a chill.

I shut my eyes and mouth 'I don't know' in silence, letting the doubt hang there, untouched and unattended, and soon it fades imperceptibly into the half-light of my mind, into the soft-serene greyness of not-knowing. And here, in the nebula of uncertainty, with a beautiful woman before me and a beautiful man in my arms, with my heart finally open to all the ambiguity and all the insecurity and all the doubt in all the world, I feel pure.

Afterword

OCD doesn't play nice; in fact it doesn't play at all. Its style is more like all-out warfare waged by a force that holds nothing back. It mobilizes the most diabolically awful weapons in the form of grotesquely disturbing images, excruciatingly painful feelings, and the deepest and most unsettling doubts that can be used against the individual. It is stealthy, virtually invisible, and relentless in its campaign. It is a most powerful adversary because it has access to, and employs the perfect source of intelligence information— the individual's own mind.

And so in Rose's remarkably brave and compelling story, we outsiders without OCD are provided an insider's view of a life under constant OCD fire. "Can it really be so?" we may ask. "Can it be so constant, so pervasive, so vivid, so raw and profane? Decidedly so!" the experts will answer. So will others with similar forms of OCD attest to the truthfulness of her account. Much of the general public knows about forms that involve obsessions associated with contaminants of various sorts, "germaphobia" for example, and the hand-washing compulsions that often are the familiar outward sign. Also widely known are obsessional concerns about personal safety that may involve checking that doors are locked, or that appliances are unplugged. However, many readers will not recognize Rose's type of OCD, the kind that is characterized by intrusive, horrific and unwanted thoughts, often of a sexual nature but just as possibly murderous, blasphemous, grotesque or otherwise shameful, guilt-inducing and frightening. The disorder comes in so many "flavors and varieties" each perfectly reflecting the individual's unique sensitivities and vulnerabilities, so there are endless possibilities.

Rose refers to her type of OCD as "pure O", though she understands that this is a commonly used but scientifically imprecise term. Pure O describes forms of the disorder in which compulsions are present, but more or less undercover. The origins of the term probably can be traced to the not-so-distant past when OCD *obsessions* were "the thoughts" and *compulsions* (rituals) were "the actions". In the last thirty or forty years it has become more widely accepted by experts that compulsions may or may not involve physical behaviors like washing or checking. Instead, it has become clear that willfully produced *mental events* can serve the same function as overt compulsions, when they serve to reduce distress about obsessions and neutralize fears about the likelihood of catastrophic outcomes. For example, a person with obsessions about becoming aligned with the Devil may, without moving a muscle, intentionally picture the smiling face of God and thus achieve some temporary relief from that fear. To Rose's credit, she understood, and accurately pointed out, that she did have a wide variety of compulsions, some overt, but many more covert "mental compulsions" in the form of checking her thoughts, memories, feelings and motivations in efforts to gain certainty about her sexual identity.

One may ask why Rose developed OCD, and why her particular form and not one of the many other manifestations of that disorder. OCD like most other psychological disorders is thought to result from both the individual's particular life experiences as well as from some inherent constitutional vulnerabilities. If two men together pick up a heavy box and one hurts his back, it was not the weight of the box (only one man was injured), nor was it the one man's biology that caused the injury (he was fine before he lifted the box). It was an interaction between the two factors. So it is with OCD.

Rose's OCD cannot be separated from her life experiences. She is the fertile soil out of which her OCD grew, the seeds of which were likely present from early on. Her descriptions of herself as a child convey the impression of a youngster with an endlessly creative mind and a boundless imagination. Her descriptions of childhood events display an early passion for life--the joy, playfulness and excitement of being young and very much alive. Those qualities exemplify the positive side of such qualities. The negative side can occur when that same mind ventures into darker and more frightening terrain. That is the realm of disaster, catastrophe and imponderable awfulness that is well within the reach of a child whose restless mind has no off-switch. The accompanying feelings can turn powerful and excruciating – fear, doubt, shame, guilt, disgust and every other form of emotional pain. As an adult, Rose retained the same essential mental and emotional qualities. In addition, her writing is a testament to her singular and exquisite visual sensibility. It makes perfect sense that her personal torment is characterized by endless, vivid images that taunted, horrified and confused her.

Rose was raised Catholic, and as many of us who were

raised within that religion, she was taught that she could sin in *thought, word or deed*. While the second and third of those stipulations were perhaps manageable to one who hopes to avoid sin, not sinning in one's thoughts can be quite a formidable challenge for busy-minded individuals. A creative, and free-ranging mind is likely to chafe against such boundaries. Combining that with the hormonal urgency of puberty meant real trouble for Rose. During the early teen years, the importance of the question "who am I?" becomes of paramount importance in the search for personal identity, and for Rose, the issue of sexual identity provided the focus for her preoccupations and distress..

Of the biological/constitutional contributions to Rose's OCD, she posits the orthodox psychiatric view that she suffers from some sort of neuropsychological dysfunction, perhaps some chemical, structural, or functional anomaly that results in "mental illness". This is viewpoint that derives from the biological model of psychological problems widely held throughout the OCD professional community. Perhaps this is so of many, maybe even most, individuals with OCD. However, my experience with thousands of OCD sufferers, many children and adolescents, makes me reluctant to label all as fundamentally flawed in their biological underpinnings. Many, particularly the children and teenagers who's conditions have not yet been complicated by many years of living with OCD do seem extraordinary, but not because they appear to me to be "broken". Like Rose, their obvious specialness seems to be more in their possession of the same sort of restless, creative, free ranging mind and fully alive emotional system rather than in any essential malfunction. As in Rose's case, their young minds ventured into questions and issues that provoked powerful unpleasant feelings for which they were ill-prepared to cope.

There is a psychological trap that is central to OCD. This trap gets sprung when the individual chooses avoidance and escape through rituals, as primary strategies for coping with the pain and pressures of the fears that captured their imagination and achieved obsessional proportions. These are the unremitting, recurring, emotionally distressing ideas, beliefs and images that drive OCD. Rose attempted to avoid many circumstances, situations and cues that triggered her obsessional images and questions about her sexuality and sexual identity. These included efforts to comfort herself through thought suppression, monitoring her body for "appropriate" reactions, and other ways of avoiding obsessional distress. When avoidance failed, she employed a variety of compulsive mechanisms in attempts to escape from anxiety generated by unwanted thoughts and images related to her sexuality. These included mental refutations, arousal tests, and varieties of forms of self-reassurance. So, like a speech phobic who manages to escape and avoid any opportunity to speak before an audience, Rose experienced fears that remained intact and became even more problematic over time. With OCD, the temporary modicum of relief provided by compulsivity, strengthens rituals and tightens the hold on the sufferer, very much like the man stuck in quicksand who struggles, only to find himself more deeply trapped by his own desperate efforts.

Roses story provides numerous details about how her efforts to solve OCD problems had gone awry. Like those of the vast majority of OCD sufferers her views of what were happening to her contained misconceptions and distortions that contributed to her problems. For example, Rose seemed to be drawn into the fiction that "true" heterosexuals (and "true" homosexuals) are capable of responding with sexual arousal to virtually all "within-category" sexual cues, while remaining physically unresponsive to cues from the opposing category. Putting oneself to such "tests" is usually doomed to failure, in part because sensations of anxiety can easily be mistaken for sexual arousal. Rose tested her reactons in an effort to pinpoint her "true sexual identity", believing at the time that she must do so, with absolute certainty, and it must be done *right now*, or she would remain miserable.

Unlike many sufferers of OCD who focus on sexual identity, however, Rose did recognize that sexual orientation is not an "either/or", categorical matter. The pioneer, sexual researcher, Alfred Kinsey, in attempting to describe sexual orientation in the general population concluded that he had to employ a seven-point scale that at each endpoint captured only the number of individuals who were "exclusively heterosexual" or "exclusively homosexual" in their orientation. Large segments of the population were represented as somewhere in between the two extremes. Rose's problem was not categorical thinking, her dilemma grew out of her efforts to fix the precise point along the dimension that she inhabited. As she came to realize the hard way, such certainty is elusive and engaging in desperate efforts to attain it are likely to end in failure. Only much later could she accept the impossibility of determining a finite point, and instead, regarded her sexual identity as a blur--a moving target.

But Rose's story has a happy ending. She was fortunate enough to have some good help in her journey to recovery. Medication alone was not to provide the answer, but it may have helped. At this point in time, clinical research indicates that the learning-based treatment known as cognitive behavior therapy (CBT) produces the most extensive and long-lasting benefits of any treatment for OCD. As Rose sought relief through psychological treatment, even the "bad" therapists in her story were not awful. They seemed smart, supportive, kind and generally skilled, but they apparently lacked the requisite knowledge of the subtleties of specialized OCD treatment, namely exposure and ritual prevention (ERP) techniques. Finally, she found a CBT therapist with the essential skills. That therapist began treatment with an emphasis on extensive psychoeducation—shaping Rose's assumptions, beliefs and expectations to provide a strong foundation for the work to follow. Then she guided Rose through a methodical exposure plan, employing critical treatment elements that have proven effective for OCD in numerous studies over 40 years of clinical research. Rose engaged her fears head on in a carefully planned, gradual, hierarchical fashion. The exposure portion of ERP was effective this time, in part because Rose was able to eliminate the rituals that undermined her previous therapy efforts. She fully accepted the profound uncertainty that underlies her existence as it does all of our existences.

For all of its formidable power, OCD is beatable when addressed with appropriate procedures and a well-prepared and courageous patient willing to face her fears head on. Rose has taken us along on her journey fraught with pain and despair but one of ultimate joy and renewal. It should inspire us all— OCD sufferers and outsiders alike. Even this, however must be tempered by her reminder that proper treatment is beyond the reach of all but a fortunate, small segment among the millions of OCD sufferers around the world. Her story provokes a question that we all might ponder: What can be done for the others?

Charles S. Mansueto, Ph.D.
Licensed Psychologist

Director, Behavior Therapy Center of Greater Washington (DC), Silver Spring, Maryland, USA
Member, Scientific and Clinical Advisory Board,
International Obsessive Compulsive Foundation (IOCDF),
Boston, Massachusetts, USA
Chair, Mid-Atlantic OCD (IOCDF Affiliate),
Silver Spring, Maryland, USA

NOTE: For more information about OCD and its treatment contact the International Obsessive Compulsive Foundation: IOCDF.org

Acknowledgements

My job here is already half done, because those who most need thanking are listed as supporters on the following pages. For once, 'I couldn't have done it without you' is literally true. So, with all of my heart, thank you. Special thanks to my boyfriend's parents, who physically went door to door to tell people about the funding campaign.

Thank you to all those on the frontline of mental health care. My therapist in New York, for saving lives. Dr Charles Mansueto, for the nice things you say about me in the Afterword which we *definitely* didn't pay you to say. OCD Action and the online mental health community, for your tireless support. I'm in awe.

Book crowd! Thanks to my agent Jonny Geller and all at Curtis Brown for taking a punt on an unknown writer. To Henry Jeffreys and Martin Baker, for mentoring me at the embarrassing first draft stage and for slipping my work under the noses of the right people. To Isobel Frankish, John Mitchinson, Amy Winchester, Miranda Ward, my phenomenally talented editor Liz Garner, and everyone at Unbound, for believing in the book, and for putting up with my obsessiveness. Your support and patience has meant the world.

More? More. Roland De Wolf. Ákos Pozsgai. Mark Cunningham. Christopher Stagg. Giles Heron. Graham Tanker. Aaron Harvey. Tom Cole. Brendan Freeman. Hilary Marshall.

And 'Eric' – one of the most generous people I've ever known – for an experience I'll never forget.

To my family, both Black Country and Breton, who are all over this book: thank you and merci. Thanks most of all to Mom and Dad, for everything. To 'Marie' for so much kindness. To 'Patty' and 'Ted' for making me into the little boy that I am today. And to my friends, for not judging me, even though I *have* thought about you naked. I love you all.

And thank you to my boyfriend, the star of the show, for trusting me to tell our story and for believing that I could get better.

Supporters

Unbound is a new kind of publishing house. Our books are funded directly by readers. This was a very popular idea during the late eighteenth and early nineteenth centuries. Now we have revived it for the internet age. It allows authors to write the books they really want to write and readers to support the writing they would most like to see published.

The names listed below are of readers who have pledged their support and made this book happen. If you'd like to join them, visit: www.unbound.co.uk.

My best friend
My Darling Emma
Anne-Marie & Bernard
Paul & Emma
Tony & Daphne
David Adam
Jessica Adams
Shira Alani
Laith Alexander
Peter Allen
Mugren Al-Ohaly
Liam Annis
Anonymous

Anonymouse
Antonia
Martin Archer
Judith Armstrong
Holly Arup
Tim Atkinson
Thomas Avery
Anna B
Martin Baker
Jason Ballinger
Laura Bambach
Tim Barber
David Barker

Amy Jane Barnes

Emily Barton

Kendra Bean

Sophie Beaumont

Antonin Beckert

Natalie Beckley

Jenny Bede

Aron Bennett

Lucy Beresford

Terry Bergin

Tom Bird

Alex Booth

James Bowman

Jo Bradshaw

Barry Smyth Bray

Martin Bretecher

Clémence Bretécher

Rose Bretécher

Daniel Bridge

Katherine Broadbent

Nicholas Brookes

Ryan Brown

Jamie Bryson

William Buckley

Bill Burdette

Oliver Burkeman

Chris Burrows

TC

Michael Caines

Jake Callaghan

Tor Cameron

Ria Campbell

Ulrika Campbell

Xander Cansell

Chloe Carter

Martin Cartwright

Matthew Cartwright

Nicola Carty

Paola Marco Casanova

Emma Cashmore

Andrew Catlin

Lois Chaber

Vera Chok

Simon Pinkerton Chuda

Tim Clark

Dominic Clarke

Katherine Clarke

Lowri Clarke

Ian Clarkson

Joe Clinton

Tom Cole

Tom Collins

Paul Comyn

Philip Connor

Allison Conroy

Bryony Cook

David Cooke

Amy Cooper

Jason Cooper

Tom Cordy

Laura Cowen

Jacob Crosby

Jordan Cross
Alex Croyle
Mikey Cuddihy
Mark Cunningham
Ashley Curry
KaitlynCurtis
Leslie Cuthbert
ID Spooner
Kat Dakin
Aine Daly
Sally Darby
Rishi Dastidar
Tora Davidson
David Dawson
Thea de Gallier
Esme Deacon
Elliot Dear
Lily Dear
Rex Dear
Phill Dearn
Kelly Decamps
Hannah Dell
JF Derry
Buck Dharma
Mark Dixon
Kate Donaldson
Rory Doona
Laura Dora
Emma Doyle
Oliver Duffy
Keith Dunbar

Yvette Earley
Kit Eaton
Kirsti Edwards
Dave Erasmus
Stephen Fairbanks
Sarah Falk
Mike Fallbrown
Clem Fandango
Andrew Faulkner
Andrew Fentham
FilthyMindedDude
Paul Fischer
Richard Fisher
Rebecca FitzGerald
Kim Fitzpatrick
Robert Fogg
Chips for the Poor
Lucy Foster
Isobel Frankish
Brendan Freeman
Timothy Frost
Lauren Fulbright
Jaclyn G.
Gaby Gabsgati
Hilary Gallo
Emma Gannon
Kim Gehrig
Kate George
Rachel Gertz
Kate Gibb
Laura Gilbert

Ruairi Gilles

Spencer Gillman

Richard Gilmour

Oisín Mac Giolla

Joshua Gleason

Ian Glover

Salena Godden

Angelique Golding

Lol Goodliffe

Keith Grady

Voula Grand

Eleanor Greatorex

Katherine Green Rosie

Andy Guest

Ian Guest

Erin H.

Gema Hadridge

Steph Hamill

Amber Hammond

Thea Hamrén

Melissa Harahan

Kelly Harding

Sean Harkin

Callum Harries

Joe Harrod

Aaron Harvey

Caitlin Harvey

Ashley Hawkins

Alison Hayday

Roxane Haydon

Abbie Headon

Ant Hearn

Patrick Hearn

Laura Herlehy

Giles Heron

Martin Hickman

Melissa Higham

Yannick Hill

Sam Hoad

Graham Hodge

Millie Horton

Matt Huggins

Alice Hughes

Jack Hughes

Lee Hughes

Andrew Hulme

Robert Hunter

Cherise Hurt

Laura Hutchinson

Christos Ioannou

Rivka Isaacson

Johari Ismail

Sam Jackson

Chris James

Richard James

Henry Jeffreys

Tom Jeffreys

Ashley Clift Jennings

Jamil Jivanjee

Elisabeth Johnson

Laura Johnson

Alice Jolly

Lucy Justice
Caroline Kahn
Victoria Kahn
Joanna Karina
Eishar Kaur
Vicky Kear
Dan Keefe
Rosie Keep
Therese Keight
Chris Kelly
Aidan Kendrick
Christina Kennedy
Anne Keyser
Dan Kieran
Laura Kiesel
Fran Kilshaw
Rosie Kinloch
Olga Kirichkova
Sophie Knock
Karen Knorr
Alex Kudlick
Louise Lamb
W TomLawrie
Jimmy Leach
Garth Leder
Amelia Lees
Raonaid Levesley
Alex Lewis
Ben Lewis
James Lewis
Rozi Leyden

Nicholas Little
James Lloyd
Kirsty Logan
Benjamin Lole
Javier Lopez
Isabel Losada
Kate Lowe
James Lowrey
Kimberley Lucas
Francis Lunn
Pauline Macavoy
Tim Macavoy
Cara Macdonald
Lynsey Mackay
Jason Mahon
Fati Mancini
Hannah Manktelow
Ellie Mann
Jon Manzoni
Catherine Marcus
Vincenzo Mariella
Dan Marks
Hilary Marshall
Daniela Martins
Abbie Mason
Felix Massie
Karen Masson
Richard Mayston
Steph McCabe
Alexandra Kate McCauley
Fiona Mcdowall

Andy McFadden

Shayne McGreal

Alice McInerney

Judy McInerney

Steven McKinnon

Jon McNaught

Caitlin Mehta

Craig Meulen

Simone Ming

John Mitchinson

Kimberly Mitton

James Moakes

Arnaud Moinet

Craig Molyneux

Ben Moran

Charles Morgan

Agathe Morisse

Emma Mullins

Louis Myles

Ellen Nabarro

Kitty Nabarro

Lee Nair

Alice Nason

Carlos Novato

Lucy Needs

Charlotte Neill

Rupert Newton

Kyle Nix

Janet Noble

E O Higgins

Charlotte Lucy O'Brien

Shara O'Brien

OCDfamilies

Georgia Odd

Chris Odedun

Tessa More O'Ferrall

Zoe More O'Ferrall

Jenny O'Gorman

Galen O'Hanlon

Ryan O'Keeffe

Suzanne Olbrich

Michele-Elizabeth Marie Oliver

Thomas Ormonde

Emma O'Rourke

Jacob Ortego

Mark Owen-Ward

Richard P

Mary San Pablo

Hannah Page

Jennifer Painter

Michael Paley

Claire Parry

Harriet Parry

Ben Pask

Rima Patel

Alex Payne

Marguerite Peck

Steve Peck

Rebecca Pedler

Adam Percival

David Perez

Robert Phillips

Oliver Pickles

Langdale Pike

Mikey Please

Anonymous Pledger

Justin Pollard

Daisy Poole

David Postolowsky

Ray Postolowsky

Harriet Potts

Ákos Pozsgai

David Prew

Paul Price

Richard Price

Tim R

Sarah Raddon

Jonathan Ratcliff

Kate Raybould

Jessica Rayner

Daniel Regan

Hillary Reitman

Jimmylee Remillard

Carmen Reumers

Ellen Richardson

Stephen Roberts

Wyn Roberts

Matt Robinson

Gerry Roche

Alexandra Roeder

Roman Virec

Roberto Rosele

Martin Round

Marilyn Ruttley

Rebecca Ryan

Tommy Ryan

Amelia Rynkowska

Rosie Bell Ryott

Christoph Sander

Jessica Sanders

Ciara Sarkar

Riccardo Sartori

Emily Sellers

Beth Selman

Anant Sharma

San Sharma

Charlie Sharp

Kari Shemwell

Keith Sherratt

Katharine Sherwood

Emily Shipp

Katie Siddons

David Simpson

Justyn Grant Singlehurst

Amalie Skovgaard

Hayley Smith

Johnny Smith

Lewis Smith

Liz Smith

Steve Smith

Erika Soliven

Rebecca Spero

C W Stagg

Janice Staines

Nathan Stanley

Carla Steele

Leon Steele

Molly Steele

Richard Stephens

Andrew Stevens

James Stevenson Bretton

SubtleBlade

Victoria Swalwell

Anne Sweeney

Neil Sweet

David T Cox

Tash Tan

Graham Tanker

Luz Tapalla

Geoffrey Taylor

Helen Taylor

Neil Xavier Taylor

Ian Thompson

Jessica Thompson

Nathan Thompson

Shannon Thomson

Simon Tierney-Wigg

Callum Tikly

Natalie Timmins

Paul Tomkins

Paul Tompsett

Kirstie Tostevin

Misti Traya

Tom Trevelyan

Victoria Trow

Edward Tucker

Mike Tucker

Stephen Tyrrell

Shaun Usher

Güldem Bilda Vaccaro

Patricia Villamor

David Virenius

Richard W H Bray

Steve Wadsworth

Nick Walpole

Lizzie Warburton

Miranda Ward

Mrs. Fee Warner

Gabriella Wass

Alice Watson

Kim Watt

Mathew Watterson

James Watts

Annis Waugh

Holly White

Lloyd Wigglesworth

Caroline Wilhelmsen

Richard Williams

Adelaide Wilson

Christine Wilson

David Wilson

Derek Wilson

Diana Wilson

Johanna Wilson

Kyle Wilson

Rose Wiltshire
Eve Wingerath
Maxine Winning
Bianca Winter
Roland Wolfe
Tom Wood
Lee Woodger
Nadia Woodhouse
Richard Woodruff

Laura Woods
Liv Woodward
Amanda Yam
Bart Yates
Danielle Youn
Robert Young
Sonya Yu
Zahariya Zahariya